Not Because it's Easy

A story of struggle, pain, and of reward on the

Tahoe Rim Trail.

David F. Maliar

Dedication:

This book is dedicated to my mother. You are the embodiment

of struggle and how it makes you strong, and that should be

celebrated. With you we all learn a lesson about life... that in

our travels, we should stop sometimes and take a deeper look;

it's with this that we can appreciate our true worth.

And to, of course, my brothers in battle, without you I would not

have made it: Steve, Greg, Paul, and John.

Contents

Prologue

"A gem is not polished without rubbing, nor a man perfected without trials" says an ancient Chinese proverb. I also read in a fortune cookie one time that, "the years teach much which the days never know." Brilliant.

Whether it comes from an ancient culture or a delicious cookie, I think the lesson here is patience in struggle; that is where true strength is born. I consider myself a patient person, at least from my own perspective. I kind of lose it though when some societally entitled brat with a great hair-do complains about how they think they have it hard, while they take a selfie on their smart phone with their middle finger in the air. Pretty descriptive, right? I know you've seen it.

I hate complainers. I complain about them all the time... It's the one thing that really grinds my gears. I won't go too far here because I know that everyone has something to complain about. I know there is a far greater number of people who have gone through far worse than I ever have. I also know that every time you grow, a new problem arises. It's all about how you prepare yourself to face it. Step number one: know that a new problem will always arise. Let's just quickly make this point and I will move on so it doesn't feel like an "uphill both ways" kind of story.

How many people in today's world actually know what it means to struggle? And better yet, how to appreciate or overcome that struggle in some way? What kind of dangers are truly present in today's world? I don't mean a bad hair day, or blistered Nintendo Thumbs because you didn't make it to the next level on the last seven attempts, and now you have to do it all over again. Or you just left the house without your cell phone and now you don't know what to do with yourself. I'm talking real struggle. I mean some good old fashioned, get your hands dirty, bloody infection, burn a hole in your pants and have to keep on going because the next water source is a grueling ten miles away... on foot... that kind of struggle.

Back in the days of the early humans, our two biggest concerns were: A: What are we going to eat? and B: What is going to eat us? They would face the problem then retreat to the cave to recover (or be dead). Now, we have to find things to fill

the stress void which are much more menial in comparison.
There are epidemics of anxiety and depression because our fight
or flight mechanisms are constantly overworked and usually for
things are aren't even all that bad. These "stresses" are
relentless. We never get a break from them so our hair turns
grey and falls out, we don't sleep right, we eat like crap, and we
think it's normal or uncontrollable. Perspective.

I think that everyone has a story to tell, but those who
have the drive to get off their couch and turn off the TV at will
are usually the ones that can say that somewhere behind them
they had a great time, they fell, they learned from it, and now
they have a great story to tell. Or maybe they somehow realized
that maybe they have a better story to tell than what has been so
they get up and go. Sometimes you write the story and
sometimes the story is written for you. You can either be a
character or an author.

Don't take things for granted. Never stop striving for
better. It's the pursuit of happiness that actually makes us
happy. Also, understand that there will always be someone out
there that had it worse and will either never get back up again or

is willing to push that much harder to get what they want. Choice. Perspective.

Let me begin my short intro story by first admitting that my perspective is not perfect. But know that neither is yours. My perspective is based on my own narrow view of the world. Perspective is what I've been able to see/experience plus what I've been told, and that equals what I believe to be true based on the thoughtful combination of the two. We are all capable of elevating ourselves and getting a different or higher perspective but it'll always be influenced by our own experiences.

I may upset a few people that are close to me with what I'm about to say and how I'm about to say it, but the only thing that I ask of those people is to please keep an open mind and to respect my perspective. Maybe someday we can discuss and bring our own takes a closer together. Elevate. And for anybody going through similar stories please understand as well for your own situations and keep an open mind for others.

I grew up in an average American family, so naturally by the time I was in 6th grade I lived with my mom and two sisters, visiting dad every other weekend. Unless of course there was something going on and he couldn't pick us up or maybe he forgot to pick us up, or had something more important to do - which may be closer to the truth.

Looking further back than that when my parents were still together we struggled... well, let's look even further back than that, before I was born. My mother, at the age of seventeen, one day discovered she was pregnant. My father, having just graduated high school and being the romantic he was, decided to ask her the big question. "So what do you think? I guess we should get married, right?" They married, my older sister was born, and their life together began. Skipping down the road you can only imagine the hard times they went through to raise a child as teenagers. A year and a half later I was born. All I can remember for the first maybe, ten years of my life was that we didn't have much. I remember having only cornbread for dinner one night and pancakes for another. "Just add water" was cheap. We were a "put a little water in the ketchup bottle to make it stretch" kind of family. Mom always made it fun.

A lot of the time it depended on how work was with dad. So that meant sometimes he would make homemade pizza or we would have steak! (It was probably more often than not venison steak from my Dad's latest hunt but that's not what we were told.) My favorite meals even today are the easiest and cheapest to make. Nothing beat Mom's shepherd's pie, nothing. It is the dinner that keeps on giving, even the leftovers are great. Eventually Dad was able to start his own concrete business and he stopped working for others. Even that was slow at times. But, the man has a work ethic like no one you'll ever meet and he became extremely successful and very much respected for his work in the industry.

My mother was, and still is today, a Registered Nurse's Assistant, caring for the elderly. It's only now that I am older that I understand and truly appreciate what my mother went through to keep us healthy and safe while working a full-time job. My father was rarely supportive growing up, as far as my perspective could see. All I wanted from him was time. He thought he needed to take us to a carnival to make us happy, but that was too expensive so often we did nothing.

I remember doing drive bys with mom, "spying" on dad, seeing if his truck was parked at The Club. The Club was a cheap basement watering hole where all the contractors would swim after work. The place smelled of cheap booze and cigars. I spent many evenings there myself begging for quarters from

Dad, Bubba, Jimmy, and John to play pinball or pool when I could barely even reach the table, as I sipped on watery Coke and ate boiled hot dogs.

When Dad was home you would have to tread lightly until you could see what kind of mood he was in, though that could change at any moment.

He would, every now and again, bring us along when he went fishing and he was actually really amazing and playful at times. But it was inconsistent. Man, he really had some swing in his moods and a really, really short fuse. I won't get into it too much. This is no woe is me bit, but I am sure you get the gist.

My mom endured a lot, but when it came to us kids it was easy for her to stand up. I remember frequent trips to Grammy's, which was more often than not a surprise, and mostly whenever daddy came home acting funny and mean. I really don't want to get into the moment's where we all knew my parent's marriage was over, but I will say it was hard for me. Really hard. A quiet kid became more quiet and more reserved. I remember thinking things over in my head a thousand times before saying them, even the simplest things. I didn't know how to express myself or if I did, I wasn't sure if it would be appropriate.

It was a very difficult time in Mom's life as well, but what really amazes me when I think about it now from an adult perspective, is how she never really let us see how much she hurt on the inside. She always did her best to make it better for us no matter the cost. I didn't know the difference then, but I do now and can only hope I am as strong for my own kids someday.

It's a sad story that could go on and on in hairy detail but I think it still proves a very good point as is. She is the definition of struggle and she has to be the strongest person that I know because of this. To have that kind of strength and love is rare. She never had any saber tooth tigers chasing her, but close enough. The way that she cares so selflessly for everybody that she meets makes her one of a kind, and if I want to write about being resilient and strong, she better be included.

Since I have grown, my dad and I have gotten much closer. He has calmed down a lot and is much more supportive with the things that I do; I can almost say that he is a totally different person. Now, he will never admit this if true, but maybe he has realized himself what is truly important. Funny what the years can teach someone, which the days never knew. Between my older sister and my younger sister, I really can't say. Perspective is your own. I guess you write your own future, or it's written for you, but either way know that it is never set in stone.

My goal in life is to fill it with as much adventure and struggle as I can, so that I can outlast anything. I don't mean put myself in abusive relationships or quit my job just for the challenge, I mean physical, get dirty, go into the unknown - kind of struggle, as much as I can handle. Backpacking, kayaking, triathlons… that sort of thing.

The following pages tell the story of five guys who set out to do just that; to find the measure of the men they thought they were and to maybe learn something about themselves as well. It's a story of struggle, of pain, of overcoming, and of reward. It's a story of lasting friendship and what it can do for the soul. It's proof that if you surround yourself with good people, you become better yourself.

I get asked all the time why I continually and deliberately put myself in a state of struggle by embarking on these journeys. I hope the answer to that question becomes inherent and more clearly understood in these words that follow, and maybe, just maybe I can help someone somewhere find their own higher perspective. Maybe this will help someone, you, get off your ass and live.

Chapter One - Where it all Begins

For my entire life, or as long as I can remember, it has been my dream to complete a long- distance hike; to walk through fields with mountains towering overhead, with days behind you and days to come. Your best friends at your side as you ford ice cold streams and while breathing the freshest air you wish you could bottle.

With the approximately 2,200 mile Appalachian Trail that extends from Maine to Georgia out of my time limits and probably my current physical capability I decided on something a little more attainable, yet still slightly out of reach… the 165 mile Tahoe Rim Trail.

Lake Tahoe is one of the largest and most beautiful alpine lakes in the world. For years it has been a prime vacation spot for skiing, boating, swimming, and a number of other outdoor activities. Next to the breathtaking vistas, this place has been a haven for outdoor enthusiasts.

With 15 downhill ski resorts, a dozen cross country ski centers, campgrounds, hundreds of miles of trails, and casinos, there is plenty to keep you occupied year round. The peak season is the summer time and activities range from sunbathing to water skiing to even cross country skiing in July at some of the higher elevations. Downhill ski resorts are open as late as April on some mountains depending on the winter they had. The Crystal Bay Visitors and Convention Bureau says that the year round population is around 50,000 while an additional 2.2 million visitors year round come for the atmosphere and recreation.

According to the United States Geological Survey, Lake Tahoe was formed as the result of geologic block faulting. Basically, the land around the lake rose up and the area that is the lake bed lowered; then with volcanic activity the mountains raised higher and higher creating a dam-like structure around the Lake Tahoe basin. This prevented water from escaping. With melt water from snow and rain carried by rivers and streams, this basin slowly began to fill until it reached its present-day level, emptying via the Truckee River.

Lake Tahoe is number two on the list of deepest lakes in the United States, second only to Crater Lake in Oregon, and the tenth deepest in the world. With an average depth of 1,000 feet and a max depth of about 1,600 feet (this changes every day) and a surface area of about 191 square miles this lake truly is awe-inspiring. It's massive.

The lake is so crystal clear that you can see to depths of 100 feet in places. With white silty sand on some of its shores, the clear water gives an almost tropical ambiance.

This region has become increasingly more popular with its newest attraction, the Tahoe Rim Trail (TRT). Completed in September of 2001 the TRT tops out at 165 miles; though I would brag that a through-hike would equal closer to 175 miles with the added distance between each of the eight trailheads. Elevations on the trail range from about 6,300 feet at Tahoe City, CA all the way up to about 10,400 on top of Relay Peak. Not the tallest peak in the region, but the highest point on the trail - the tallest being Freel peak (10,881 feet).

The TRT winds around spectacular ice-cold alpine lakes, beautiful forests with towering conifers, wide open summits and valleys packed with beautiful wildflower meadows.

Moving through the states of Nevada and California, with its constant changes in elevation, the trail provides an opportunity to see an extremely diverse and ever changing environment.

The west side of the lake sees considerably more precipitation than the east. Its high peaks trap the clouds as they struggle to conquer the climb, dumping their load of rain, sleet, or snow along the way. Because of this effect the eastern side of the lake stays much drier throughout the year.

The trail was designed to follow mostly ridges and peaks and at certain times of the year on the east side of the lake it is common not to find a water source for a half a day or more. In the later summer months you could go days without so much as a puddle to replenish your water supplies.

The trail was designed to accommodate equestrians, mountain bikers, and of course those who dare to venture out on foot. The Lake Tahoe region is a very popular site for mountain bikers from around the country and there are various tournaments and races held each year.

After learning so much about this place, the TRT seemed perfect for my time and distance constraints, and the pictures and descriptions I saw on the internet and in the guide book made me fall in love with the idea of doing this hike. I called my good friends Paul and Greg, twin brothers and the type that would express interest in such a thing. I also mentioned it to my long-time friend Steve who happened to be my roommate at the time. The plans were underway. We had a fellowship of sorts. A few months later Greg mentioned that a friend and coworker of his, John, was interested in coming along. I was cool with that but I didn't want to go any higher than five for the sake of pace and supplies. He was ambitious (so Greg said), he worked out every day to prepare (Greg said), he's a real great guy and fun (Greg said). And then Greg said he had no experience at all backpacking.

OK, not a big deal, we could make up for his lack of knowledge in the outdoors, and as long as he was in shape we would be fine. It turned out that he wasn't actually a tender-footed Canuck when it comes to outdoors as we all had thought, but did he really know what he was getting into?

Well, to tell you the truth I really had no idea what I was getting into. Even with all my years of Boy Scouts and miles on other trails to back me up, this trail was a challenge even I was not ready for.

Like I mentioned before, my mom always did her best to provide for me and did her best to make sure I turned out the best I possibly could, considering the struggles. The answer to how I turned out is debatable but I think that I pretty much came out on top, and my mom says I'm cool, so...

She signed me up for the Cub Scouts when I was really little and later I moved up the ranks and on to the Boy Scouts. If not for the path she set me on I could have been a much different person right now. I think about the choices I was faced with and to think that if I didn't have such positive influences I really could have gotten myself into trouble. But I digress again.

Because of the Boy Scouts, and all of my own personal adventures growing up, I am no stranger to the outdoors. In fact when there was a campout or a party in the woods with friends back in my high school days I was usually the one who tended the fire and cared for those attempting the daring stunt of fire jumping or other such idiotic things. You have to have respect for fire if it's something you are looking to enjoy. I've always had that respect, understanding the devastation it could potentially cause.

Being the at ease type, a lot of the times at those parties I was the one to volunteer for the 10 minute trip by myself, with no flashlight, all the way to the dark dirt driveway to pick up a few late comers to the party.

My comfort in the outdoors is less because I know the difference between an Ash and an Elm tree, and more because of what the outdoors was able to provide me growing up. From what you have learned about me so far, it should be understood well enough that I have had my share of troubles as a child. Whenever I needed to escape the civil war at home or the drama of having two sisters, I walked away, and usually right towards nature. There is a certain kind of loneliness in the woods that makes the crowds of life disappear and fills you with a new sense of commotion. The wind, the animals, the dim hum of civilization from beyond the treeline. There's no judgment out there, and especially in the dark, at night. It's perfect.

I live for that high that nature provides so I make it a point to get out no matter what life throws at me. I had been hiking hundreds of times, camping thousands, and had been in the woods for a week at a time with no problem. I know I could be prepared to survive in the wilderness if I needed to; much better than the average person anyways. And besides, I have the wilderness survival merit badge to prove it…

Now the problem that I underestimated was that I have never had the combination of the two activities (camping and hiking) for more than a long weekend. How much harder could it be going 15 to 20 miles a day on treacherous terrain? I was about to find out. The following pages include writings directly transcribed from my trail journal. Well at least the words I could read. My handwriting is horrendous. These entries are written in *italics.*

Chapter Two - The Beginning of Struggle

We just flew in from Stewart Airport in New

York. We landed here in Chicago around 2:30 Central time and

it is where I purchased this Journal. The flight in was normal,

like most flights I guess, with only a few bumps along the way.

We were all scattered throughout the plane; I think Greg and

Paul were the only ones who got to sit together. It was a lonely

flight to say the least. Obviously there's a flood of thoughts

going through my head. There's no way of telling how this trip

will be on the mind, on the body, on the soul... on our

friendships. I am excited and scared all at the same time. John

seems pretty cool like Greg described. I think he'll be perfect

for our 5th man.

Unforgettable. No matter what happens this

trip will be unforgettable. I miss Cassie already, but like she

said, she'll be there when I get back. I only wish I wasn't missing her birthday. What a horrible boyfriend I am. Although (not to make this sound worse than it is, me not being there for her) this is like living a dream I've had since I was a little boy. I don't think anything will get in the way of making this the most memorable experience possible.

Here's to a safe trip and the best friends anyone could ask for. It starts here...

July 1st 2006   5:06 pm - Pacific Time

"I could feel each cheek pass by my cheeks as she walked by, I could feel the division!" Greg whispers as the middle aged, though very attractive flight attendant passes by. I guess you would have to know him to find that funny, it was more in the way he said it. Just a little taste of what we are to experience on this trip I am sure.

We just passed over the Rocky mountains and the little boy behind us continues to cry for mommy, then for daddy, then he's freezing, then for mommy, and then finally for daddy again before he falls asleep; just to repeat the process in another half hour or so I am sure. Poor Steve has the abnormally large man

23

reclined in front of him reading what seems to be a printout of a

forwarded email that is of "little known facts." Did you know

that to hide bullet holes in the wall of your hotel room you can

use tooth paste? I hope I don't need to know that.

   An hour maybe until we touch down in Reno. The view

of the mountains is unlike anything I have ever seen before. So

THIS is what mountains look like! And we thought we had these

things back in Connecticut. They are enormous, snow capped

(in JULY), and jagged; unaffected by as much glacial erosion as

those mole hills back home. By now I am tired of sitting,

starting to get a headache, and in desperate need of food. Good

thing for the view. We'll be there soon!

   July 1st 2006   11:23 pm - Pacific Time

   So that caged rat feeling that I was beginning to get on

the plane? It disappeared faster than it came when the view

began to open up and clear through the clouds as we prepared

to land in Reno, NV. It's a wide open place with an

overwhelming view. Reno was exactly as I imagined it would be... as least from what I can remember from that show Reno 911 on Comedy Central.

The drive to the lodge where we are spending our first night was a spectacular tour through the mountains, scarred by past forest fires. The final pass between two peaks opened up at Tahoe City, CA where our hike will begin. The lodge is okay. More like a cheap motel in the woods. Nothing like the picture online.

And HOLY PINECONES! Probably the largest pine cones that I have ever seen. Like the size of Steve's head! Everything around here is so big and so beautiful. We walked into town to get some dinner at a lakeside restaurant, Jakes I believe it was called. My last burger for some time I am sure. The walk back to the "lodge" was probably the most motivational part of this beginning. The stars alone are enough to make you realize that you are at someplace special, far from our home with its skies polluted with light. It hits us, what we are really about to do. We can see the mountains in the distance through the light of the moon, some of which snow-capped, and a faint sense of fear surrounds us, at least I think it's fear... anxiety or anticipation maybe?

Tomorrow morning we go pick up our permits and last minute supplies, breakfast, then our first day on the trail; a solid 16.3 miles according to Paul who is the designated map guy. Greg is the motivational speaker, Steve the medic, and I am the cook. I don't think John got elected a position really, I'm sure we'll find something. What are we getting into? We need a medic? Let's get some sleep.

Chapter Three - Introductions

I first met Steve in the summer of 1996. I had just moved to the opposite end of town, and I didn't really have many friends in the neighborhood. OK, so I didn't have any friends at all. So during the long summer months when I was out of school you would see me doing one of two things by myself; from 1-5 pm you would find me at the local town pool polishing my skills on the diving board, or I could also be found down by the river fishing or just screwing around exploring. I built many tree forts in those woods with wood and nails I would "find" in the area and surrounding yards. The river itself was always best when the dam was closed upstream and the water level dropped. The water level would drop so low and leave nothing but a few scattered pools were the fish would settle, making it like shooting fish in a barrel. My record was 61 fish in an hour catching anything ranging from 2 inch sunfish to 3lb bass!

Though most of my time was spent on the Farmington River, it was at Welch Pool where I met Steve. He was a lifeguard, and actually one of the guys that convinced me to join the boy's high school swimming and diving team once I got to high school. I had no idea there was a competitive world out there with the sport. Being at the pool for so long every day without fail, I got to know the life guards quite well and most of them were only a few years older than I. I was often the first one at the gate when it opened and the last one to go home when it closed, (rain or shine).

One of my first memories of Steve was when he paraded himself into the pool area one oppressively hot and humid day wearing a shirt with the sleeves cut of. Now, I'm not talking cut off at the seems, I mean Muscle Man, USA style where the whole side of the shirt got blown out. Everyone had a good laugh and especially when he explained the shirt as needing "something on the lighter side of air conditioning." He certainly was no muscle man. He was pretty much a dork, I think that's why we got along so well. Since then Steve and I have become very good friends. I even ended up having my first beer with Steve. But my mom is probably going to read this so I won't say more.

Steve and I frequently ventured out on day hikes in the local state parks and every now and again we would splurge on a trip somewhere farther away. Mt. Monadnock and Mt. Washington in New Hampshire were some of our favorites.

Mt. Washington is the tallest, and arguably most difficult peak to climb in the Northeastern United States, but still not higher than the lowest elevation in the Lake Tahoe region, just to put things in perspective. *The most difficult as long as you don't cheat and drive up the road or take the cog rail, that is.

Steve and I, and other friends, would build fires in the woods near my house with "campsites" to surround them. Really it was just an excuse to have a little not-so-legal under-aged fun. The older we got the more we dreamed. We both have an innate sense of adventure that seems to grow with every trip.

After he graduated from college he made plans to go with his cousin on a little hike known as the Long Trail. To sum it up, it goes from Canada to Massachusetts through the hills of Vermont. It takes the average hiker going about ten miles a day about one month to complete. Not an easy task by any means. He made it about five days and had to quit due to injuries and fatigue. Toenails falling off and bleeding from the feet (and his 60lb pack) will do that to you. Yes that's what I said, a SIXTY POUND backpack. He knows now it's not a good idea to bring a hatchet with you on a distance hike.

His determination for finishing the TRT is apparent; it's almost like redemption. There was no way that would happen again. This time around it's just a matter of preparing more carefully and wearing the right boots. Our objective was to go no slower than 15 miles a day with a few 20 milers to brag about, so this would be no easy feat.

At the time of the TRT trip, Steve was a PE teacher in our home town of Windsor, CT. He is now the Chief Operating Officer for a small family business.

John, I didn't know much about. The first time I met him was at the airport heading to Reno. He is a friend of Greg's from when he worked in New York City as an investment banker. I know after the hike he will be doing some traveling in Israel among other places. The Canadian native gets his sense of adventure from snowboarding and skiing and has an extremely strong drive to succeed in whatever he does. Greg always spoke very highly of John and I was eager to meet him.

Greg and Paul. There's so much I can say about these two it is difficult to know where to begin. I remember an article written about them in the local town newspaper that was titled, "Brothers are Exemplary." That pretty much said it all. It went on to explain how great they were, how smart they were, and all the while balancing three varsity sports in high school; the top of their class these two. Now, I hope this comment is correct and doesn't start a battle, they have always been very competitive, but I think Paul was one place ahead of Greg in the class ranks when it was all said and done.

I met them on the swim team at Windsor high school. My first year I didn't really get to know them all that well, but I really remember was losing a meet by just a few points because they were on a family vacation in Florida. Had they been at that meet we would have CRUSHED the competition. I was the typical nerdy outcast who really kept to himself, nerdy without the good grades though. I really didn't have a reason; I wasn't a loser or anything. At least my mom said so, remember? I just kept a lot hidden. Sitting back and watching the fools go 'round. A wallflower of sorts. Truth be told, I didn't think anyone really liked me at all. I was so nervous joining that team. I had butterflies in my stomach all day long leading up to the first team meeting after school. Everyone seemed to know someone except for me.

After a few years of knowing these two, Paul one day admitted that they used to call me names behind my back. Not in a bad way at all. They called me Clark Kent. Remember, I was that nerdy- glasses- long haired- scrawny boy who didn't know how to swim a lick... but then I got better. I was determined. That geeky boy in the hall suddenly became a different person when the glasses came off and the pressure was on. Those guys were my encouragement to come out of my shell. I never really had confidence in myself until someone actually had faith in me and respected what I could do. I give them this credit wholeheartedly. I think it is because of them that I excelled at swimming and diving the way that I did. I'd even go as far as saying that encouragement spread through every aspect of my life.

We would have those parties I mentioned in the woods behind their house, and of course I was the one who designed the fires. Oh, we had some good ones. The next morning we would look around at the new clearing around us, void of any downed branches with a rusty old axe lying somewhere nearby; it was all consumed by the flame which lasted into the early morning hours. The 30 acres of land that surrounded us was quiet. It was private. We were hardly ever bothered out there by the neighbors or the police.

Those were the best times and whether they know it or not Greg and Paul were some of the first to actually accept me the way that I was. I never had to put on an act and I loved that. I despised those who felt that's how they must live their lives, always playing a part in some stupid play, like they had something to prove. But it turns out that most everyone is afraid to really express themselves at that age. We all just show it a little differently, I guess. Greg and Paul just have this ability to be so non-judgmental and genuine and that brings out the best in everyone around them. True leaders.

Greg went on to graduate from Columbia University and worked in real estate investment in New York City, and has since been transferred to Brazil and is basically The Man (official title). Paul Graduated from the University of Pennsylvania and taught bilingual social studies in the city as well. Prior to this trip Paul completed his second master's degree in international relations at Georgetown University in Washington DC and has gotten a job with the Foreign Aid Commission and will be stationed in Tel Aviv, Israel. Achieve much? I have the utmost respect for these two.

As far as experience in the outdoors: Paul gave himself a crash course in hiking when he decided one day to hike in and out of the Grand canyon, by himself; and a learning experience it was. What was his first multi-day hike, actually turned out to be one of the best experiences of his life. Naturally he needed more. Greg on the other hand, not so much. His experience goes as far as a couple days in the Delaware water gap with Paul a year earlier, that and the time he spent in the woods growing up on the 30 acres. Not that he's a fool, just a little new when it comes to knowing what to expect.

But Like I said, it's not like any of us really knew what to expect... at all.

Chapter Four - Day 1

July 2nd 2006 3:20 pm – Pacific Time

We had a little bit of a late start this morning but we are on our way. Right now we are resting at Lake Watson about 5 hours into it. Here we can top off our water supplies and freshen up a bit.

This morning we had a little trouble getting to the campground where we were to pick up our permit to enter Desolation Wilderness, which actually isn't until about day 6 of the hike. We planned on taking a cab to the campground but all services were completely booked for the next hour. Where are we? What do they have, one cab out here?

We couldn't wait that long and still stay on track. After about ten minutes of wasted time, John and I decided to rent bikes and pedal our way there. We pumped out 5 miles in 32 minutes, uphill both ways, including time to fill out paperwork... not too shabby!

So we got going around 10:30 in the morning, maybe.

And not like the bike story which was a little exaggeration... this

was UPHILL; and tomorrow will be just the same. This is by no

means easy. But remember like Paul said 4 months ago being

the history buff he is, we do these things, "NOT BECAUSE

THEY ARE EASY, but because they are hard; because that goal

will serve to organize and measure the best of our energies and

skills, because that challenge is one that we are willing to

accept, one we are unwilling to postpone, and one we intend to

win ... " - John F. Kennedy Jr.

July 2nd 2006   9:16 pm – Pacific Time

It's good to see that everyone shares the same

excitement that I do. This day proved to be challenging to say

the least, but also a learning experience for these days to come.

I've learned that it's too hot for my boots and sweaty feet will

cause blisters. It's the first day and I already have 5. We

weren't on the trail for 20 minutes when I got my first hot spot

on the back of my heal. The best decision I could have made was to bring my TEVA *sandals, I may end up needing them on a more permanent basis rather than just around camp.*

On a side note... as we sit here around the fire, everyone near about let loose their bowels when a rather rambunctious coyote decided to let us know he was upon us with an eardrum popping yip and howl. I am assuming it was a coyote but it very well could have been a wolf with the way it howled. It didn't sound like a Connecticut coyote, that's for sure. We were mid conversation when I heard a siren in the far distance and thought it was an animal, but when we heard and actual an animal, we really got em caught in a bunch.
Back to the day.

We did about 17.5 miles today and through some of those wild flower fields I read about in the trail guide. A little more than what we had planned to do, but we figured we might need the head start later.

What a beautiful sight those meadows were, and just as the sun began to fade behind the mountains. It was late in the season but a lingering smell of sweet pollen filled our senses; this is why we are here. That stop at Watson Lake was well deserved and very much needed. I don't think we could have made it this far without it. It was a small lake (more like a pond) where we restocked our water and were able to dip our already aching feet. Wasn't THAT cold, but boy did it feel good. Serine is the only way to describe it, really, especially the way the light just peeked through the tree, illuminating the faint fog that was beginning to settle around the water.

Long conversations with Greg and Paul really make me understand that this trip means as much to them as it does to me. Maybe for different reasons but it seems we are all in it as a part of transition (Greg starts his new job in July) or for some sort of personal gratification, like we are trying to get much more out of it than just walking 165 miles just for fun. The challenge of today and tomorrow's literal 17-mile uphill trek will prove what we are made of. Today, even dehydrated and hurt, we still made it through. The support that the five of us will provide along the way (and these trials) is what will get us through to the end. Basically, I believe if we can get into a groove and learn from mistakes, we will make it. Just keep moving the feet, no matter how much they hurt.

We really had no idea what to expect after that first day. It seemed that every corner we sluggishly peeked around had a new challenge to face. One thing that I thought was a good idea, and I am glad I thought of it before it was too late, was to get a written reaction from each of the other four the first night and then again the last night. I wanted to see what everyone else thought and how they felt. I wanted to see how those thoughts would be different at the end, or would they be the same?

To define struggle I think we have to look at what it means in a literal sense before we can go throwing that word around. Good old Webster (who happened to be from my home state of Connecticut, actually a town I used to live in!) defines it as:

"**1 :** to make strenuous or violent efforts in the face of difficulties or opposition <*struggling* with the problem> **2 :** to proceed with difficulty or with great effort <*struggled* through the high grass> <*struggling* to make a living>"

"To proceed" and 'violent efforts", I would be safe in saying that those statements pretty much define what we are about to throw ourselves into, with some "tall grass" too. Our feet had just gotten wet and pretty soon we'll be in over our heads. The question still remains, however... why? Yeah, because it is hard... but why? For me it was a dream, a dream come true.

John –

"Whatever doesn't kill me, will only make me stronger."

Greg –

"Today we learned many things, most importantly the value of water. It only proves that both physical and mental preparations are not enough: there are certain things that must be present. Also, though the [items to bring] draft was important, we still brought way too many superfluous items. This is 1000 times harder than I thought it would be... making victory that much sweeter!!"

Paul –

"I thought to myself that this trip would be decided in the first day. We had missteps, near death-by-thirst, and a negative vibe towards the Tahoe area. But as Watson appeared in the distance we found that we are strong! We're a feisty bunch that, through defining struggles, proves its mettle and it's true worth. This trip will succeed and I know this because I know the men that sit around this fire now, bloodied, but unbowed."

Steve –

"Well, it was a tough first day out here in Tahoe. Hard for me anyways... the other guys seemed to be cruising along fine. I was OK on the flats and downhills, but the uphill climbs were killing me. Not so much my leg strength, it was fine. But cardio-wise I was hurting. I'm pathetically out of shape. But I'll live. After what happened on the LT [Long Trail], I am not quitting this hike. It'll get me in shape. Tomorrow is all uphill and will be very difficult. But after that, if I make it through day 2 it should get easier. My pack is heavy. Nevertheless, it is

awesome out here. The views are spectacular. Hopefully I can dump some weight in the bag at the store. It is so beautiful out here... I will make it through this trip!

P.S. I'm really glad Dave was able to put this together and experience a dream of his.

P.S.S. The coyote/wolf that came right close to our camp Scared the shit outta me. It was cool though."

It's funny how perspective is different between the group members; though we all shared the same feelings pretty much… it's hard, and we wanted it! But the way we battled up and down the mountains, through the snow, the desert, the swamp, the rivers, and the sand, the way each of us viewed it is completely different. It's about putting things in your own perspective and facing the challenge that is put in front; as well as the struggles of the group.

Chapter Five - Day 2

July 3rd 2006   6:00 am – Pacific Time

Our little friend came back last night. I don't know what time it was but my guess would be around 2am when we heard the howl. Then nothing. Then again, then closer, and then like it was right next to the tent! I really wasn't as scared this time (though I did sleep with the wooden club that I found to scare him off with the first time he came around... had he gotten any ideas for round 2 I'd'a busted him!) I almost half expected it to return though, that's why I started passing out those clubs before we went to sleep. As far as I know there was only one. I kept thinking that the one we heard was the diversion while the others circled around their prey, getting into attack position. Damn you Discovery Channel! You are always giving me just a little too much information.

I didn't really sleep that well last night anyways, especially since our good friends of the wild kept waking me up.

It got so cold. 85 degrees during the day isn't bad but up at an elevation this high, it gets cold at night. There are a few things that I will have to change tonight when I sleep, another great learning experience. Like instead of bringing the one pound sleeping bag because it was lighter, splurge for the heavier one for warmth. Not like there's too much I can do about it now, but more clothing layers will have to do I guess.

I got out of the tent about a half hour ago and rebuilt the blaze with the remaining heat from the embers left by last night's blaze. It just needed a quick oxygen fix, a little kindling, and it was keeping me warm again. I just hope it warms up quickly like it did down in Tahoe City yesterday. The morning sun is beginning to shine through and the smoke from my fire paints vertical lines on a stone wall (evidence of a farming effort many years before we made this spot our camp). A rather large chipmunk perched himself up on top of the wall, stretching before he begins his daily ritual of gathering I am sure. The only other thing I am wondering now is how many other animals are we going to run into on the trail?... this was only the first night! Hopefully it will all be chipmunks and squirrels.

Let's find something to compare today with so far.

Right now I am writing and walking at the same time. Not too

much time to rest. The only thing that can compare is working

for my dad stripping a foundation, just me and him, on that 115

degree day two years ago. (He's a concrete guy.) Still only 85

out here today and the only thing missing is the headache and

the puking. But the effort is surely there. We get through this we

win.

Oh my god where do I begin? We decided to camp

tonight a little early at Mud Pond. It wasn't too muddy, actually

quite clear but I guess this is a seasonal pond that usually dries

up by the end of August, probably a little muddy by then. With

all the damn snow that is up here I can't see it ever drying up.

And my god is this location beautiful! The pond lies in the

center of a gully, surrounded on all sides by a very steep incline.

We managed to find a flat enough spot on the bottom to set up

45

camp; probably a pile of sediment carried down the slope to be spread out here at the bottom. The evidence is clear as the trees of the slope are forced to bend away from the incline as they grow, due to the weight of the icy avalanches of the winter season. We are currently at an elevation of about 9,800 ft.

Being surrounded by these mountainous walls, at least we are protected from the wind. The fire that I made tonight was a real pain to keep going. It was so hard to get warm. First I blame it on the crappy wood that is up here and second the lack of oxygen. We really feel the effects of the altitude when we start to get out of breath, which is quite often to say the least. Especially for us Connecticans! I managed a little while ago to get a cell phone signal on top of the ridge so I could call Cassie just to let her know that I was still alive. It was so good to hear her voice.

Tomorrow we will hit the highest point on the trail at about 10,400 ft. SO high up! Relay Peak I believe it's called. I think because it is where the radio relay towers are placed, a high enough location to send it in all directions. Relay peak is the highest point in the northern lake region according to our maps.

So much happened today I don't even know where to begin. All day I thought of millions of things to write about but had very little time to write it down. I hope I can remember most of it.

I decided a while back that my boots were not the best option for me with all the sweating and rubbing and swelling and throbbing so I broke down and started to wear my sandals. I didn't want to resort to that, but I really had to. My blister count is up to 9 this evening, so I think it's a good switch. Needless to say at this point my feet are in rough shape. And with all this snow it is making my feet cold and wet so either way I loose. I will try and wear my boots again if it gets too bad out there but it really hurts now to even put them on. I don't know what to do.

All the frogs just stopped peeping... right now we are in eerie silence. I thought it sounded eerie when they started, but we soon got used to them as the sound took over our senses. It was loud, there must have been a million of them. Now, nothing.

This silence means 1 of 3 things. It's mating season and they all just got laid, John scared them quiet with his snoring, or there's a possible predator. For all our sakes (and that includes the frogs) I hope they're getting laid.

Anyways, we started out the day knowing what we were in for just by looking at the map... somewhat knew what we were in for I mean. At this point I would like to more officially say that today was the most physically taxing day of my life. I can at least say the same for Steve as well. It was about 75% uphill and towards the end, 25% uphill in the snow. The snow made it hard to even find the path at times. I'm talking ten feet in some places! I think I kept an OK pace; you really get into a rhythm going uphill, even with 30 lbs on your back. It's when you stop that you feel the hurt and it makes it that much more difficult to get going again... don't break the rhythm!

As much as I couldn't expect the difficulty, I could in no way expect or even imagine it would be this beautiful here. That really fast climb today presented us with some amazing views. Jaw dropped and in complete awe I would look out and away from the path and see 3000 ft down to the lake and everything that surrounds it. At times we would walk along a steep incline, and if you slipped off the path and fell, you would roll for a really long time until you came to a stop on either a pile of rocks or a copse of trees. Don't fall! That's it.

Once we started to reach the end of the day it opened up into the alpine zone where there are no trees and we could see many of the formations that made these mountains so high. Apparently these were all once volcanic. Every now and again we would run into a laccolithic butte . This is what's left when magma would seep through cracks in sedimentary rock and harden only to have the softer rock surrounding erode away in time.

Silent frogs again. I didn't even hear them start up again. I think I am just going to try and get some sleep before I get too paranoid. Another long day tomorrow... I HOPE I can get some sleep. The only thing really frightening me about the trail is the incredible amount of snow that we can see on the opposite side of the lake. Will we be able to find the path? How will my feet hold up? Will I be forced to use my boots? OK bed time, my arm is falling asleep laying in this position anyways. Maybe I'll remember more about today, tomorrow. Damn Frogs again...

Chapter Six - Life and Death Struggle

As much as it is good for you to choose to struggle through something for the experience and strength, sometimes you don't have too much of a choice at all. Sometimes the struggle could even mean life or death. Either way, if you can find the strength and courage to make it through, you suddenly realize that maybe certain things in life aren't impossible. And I'll tell you what, it can really change your perspective on things.

I was driving down Interstate Highway 84 on June 27th 2005 on my way home from a springboard diving clinic in which I was the instructor. I remember being at about the rock quarry which is visible to the right of the highway. They actually deleted a mountain from the scene, that's amazing to me.

It was about 3:00 pm and I was about 15 minutes of normal driving with normal traffic from the Division I University where I worked as their diving coach. I got a phone call from my friend who also worked with the team. She was one of the first friends I made in college and at that point we both had just recently graduated from the same university where we were both now employed.

She called to let me know that it was probably not a good idea to enter the pool through the main lobby doors. To enter through the back door because the press was out there and the boss thought it would be good to not say anything at this time. It would be best to avoid them. My only response was "… and why is that?" She didn't know that I didn't know.

I made it back to the school in about 5 minutes flat with white knuckles and a sore throat from screaming with such anger and sadness that I am sure the cars next to me heard and felt my pain. I was by myself and didn't want to be anymore. She had just told me that one of our friends, a recent graduate and former team captain of the swim team, was in the intensive care unit at the Hospital and no one was sure if she would make it through the rest of the day.

We knew she had problems with her on and off again, now ex-boyfriend but we never thought it would go that far. The previous evening when she got home, after spending the night with friends, she got a visit from her ex. His ignored calls were relentless all that evening. He came to her suburban apartment with a backpack that contained a change of clothes (which he kept outside) and a knife... that he kept on him as he entered.

It was the most gruesome act of violence that could be imagined. It is hard for me to think that the human mind is capable of such things. It is not my story to tell in such detail so I will stick to the basics, and the results. The results from my perspective anyways.

Her roommate at the time ultimately saved her life by calling 911, but the paramedics that responded were able to bring her back to life. The courage and knowledge coupled with their ability to act is nothing short of heroic. A huge credit goes to them and their quick response. Without those that responded I don't want to even think of what could have been.

She survived the brutal attack and after a long and grueling recovery, went on to finish her student teaching requirement that fall. She earned her degree and currently works as an elementary school teacher.

Wearing her 20+ scars almost proudly she faces the world everyday with a determination and grace that is unmatched by anyone I am sure to ever meet. There are permanent physical and psychological effects but she makes it work and still succeeds. You can't help but respect her. She was always a beautiful girl and now the glow of life in her eyes just amplifies that beauty.

I started coaching at the university while still a student myself, so she and I are around the same age and were friends from when I was still on the team. She is currently married to an amazing man and has since had a child. Modern medicine is like magic as far as I'm concerned.

We can all say what we are doing is impossible or that sometimes the pain, whatever the pain, is too much to bare but really you need to just be strong and take the time to learn from it. Keep perspective, gain perspective, elevate perspective.

I know in my friend's case, she lives every day like she were dying, like the Tim McGraw song that I caught her admiring one day. Live life to its fullest every day and you will never be unfulfilled. Disappointing or destructive things may happen, but try and find the good in it and you will soon understand that everything can have a purpose. If she can live such a happy and fulfilled life, anyone can.

Now I am sure you are wondering what happened to the scum bag that was responsible. The police responded and were able to subdue him after he superficially began to cut himself. The coward didn't have the strength or courage to cut deeper. He is currently in jail with a chance for parole, and could very well be let out in a rather short amount of time. Let me get personal for a second. All that jazz I just said about living life to the fullest... nevermind, let me keep that one to myself as well.

She is a huge inspiration to me in a everything that I do. It gives me perspective and the strength to share that perspective the best I can. I will always be there for those that I love, even if space and time divides us. She affected me so much that later in life I decided on moving forward with a career in law enforcement where I am still today. I hope one day I can be there for someone the way they were there for her, though I also hope I never have to be.

(Thank you for everything.)

Chapter Seven - Day 3

July 4th 2006   7:23 am – Pacific Time

Another cold, uncomfortable night with very little sleep.
Tune strange thing though is that I really haven't felt tired yet.
Normally, I sleep until 8 or 10 in the morning then drag myself
to work but I really have yet to feel sleepy, not even once. Here I
wake up around 5am after sleeping on and off for a total of
maybe two hours, and then roll around in the tent for a good
half hour in the single ray of light before I quit and go out to
begin breakfast. Steve says that it's probably the adrenaline and
excitement, I could agree with him I guess. It could also be the
crappy, too short sleeping bag and no sleeping pad. One of
these nights though I am sure to crash and burn.

I feel good though, I guess. Not too sore considering
our trek so far. I think I am going to continue walking in my
Tevas, just with double socks for warmth and protection. Last
night I decided to clean my socks in mud pond. Doesn't sound

too smart considering the name, but it worked, and holy cold!

Could it be the hardened snow drift that was cascading into the

pond that makes it this way? (Sarcastically of course) Its colors

are brilliant as the snow changes from white to aqua marine

through the frigid water. Yeah, ice-cold, like pins and needles

cold, followed by instant numbness. I couldn't figure out how

the whole pond wasn't frozen over. It felt great on my swollen

feet though.

So according to Paul, the map guy, today should be a

quick uphill to relay peak, then a much welcomed descent for the

remainder. Hope the feet hold up!

July 4th 2006   10:43 am – Pacific Time

It's July 4th, Happy Birthday Cassie!!! I almost forgot

what day it was until I wrote it down for the second time today.

Snow... snow... snow... We just took about 30 minutes

to try and find the trail and another 15 to decide that we

couldn't take the path once we figured it out. It was like a scene

from a bad Sylvester Stallone movie where we decided to slide

down the snowy mountain on our backs to escape the inherent danger above with villains in our wake. For a second we debated taking out the sleeping pads and sliding down on them like sleds, but we didn't have time or the patience to pack them back up when we were done. And I don't have one, remember? It was a cleared avalanche path with toppled trees and piles of snow at the bottom. The only problem now after having the most fun I've had in the snow since I was maybe 12, is that we now have to climb back up the same distance we just descended. Looking at the brighter side this option would actually save us hours. Either way this climb up to Relay Peak is turning out to be a little more than just a quick ascent to the top.

July 4th 2006   12:51 pm – Pacific Time

OK, this snow is getting just a little ridiculous and there are literally no trail markers to be seen. The combination of no signs of trail and failing to stop and figure it out, we went straight up the steepest side of what will be the tallest peak on this stroll rather than hitting the switchback. Steve says "the man way" as he near about goes into cardiac arrest. Now I am really feeling the burn. We stopped again because Paul just ran

ahead to try and find our missing trail. Yeah, ran ahead. He's
out of his mind if you ask me, but as long as we get there in once
piece. And better him than any of us. He's clearly in the best
shape.

Almost to the top, it should be downhill after that so at
least it will get easier. Oh and to top it all off the air is thinner,
which makes it harder to breath. My guess is that we are at
10,000 feet above sea level and about 100 feet from the path.
But why would anyone listen to the guy with the most map
experience? Who assigned these jobs! Oh yeah, me...

I don't want this to be a journal of complaints but it's
better than bringing someone else down with me. I should really
write about the views, which, by the way, keep getting better and
better even though the trek becomes more difficult as the eternal
seconds crawl by.

Mood swing.... Being Independence Day we are caught
every now and again singing patriotic songs to lift the spirits
and try to keep them high. Thanks to our motivational
speaker/singer, Greg. This was quite a change from our usual
songs... adult contemporary mostly. You tend to lose your mind

a little, see? And then there are the conversations about our problem with gas! I'm not talking Exxon or Mobil either. It's either because of the altitude or something we ate, but I have never in my life seen 5 more gaseous men.

July 4th 2006   9:31 pm – Pacific Time

A lot of entries today, but we also had a lot of downtime for writing/ trail rediscovery. Nonetheless we still covered almost 18 miles. Today was not only the most difficult day we've had so far (and probably/hopefully/maybe for the remainder of the trip) but I can also see it as a chance to prove just how serious we are about doing this. Like I said, we had no idea what we were to expect, and now I'd say we have a really good idea what we are in for.

Today has also shown us that we are in fact strong enough physically and mentally to conquer this possibly life altering walk. I say that we have passed the test. Bruised and broken, we will make it.

Off in the distance we can hear the fireworks displays around the lake. In the local paper back at the "lodge" on our first night at Lake Tahoe, we read of maybe 4 or 5 displays they were going to happen at different times around the lake. Too bad they are all out of our view. A mountaintop view would have been something to remember.

The fourth of July. This day and this weekend are usually a time to be with family and celebrate our freedom. Though the family I am with right now is equally as important to me, and all the while we celebrate our freedom in a rather unique way, there's still that something missing. Barbecues, beers, and family brawls. What a great nation we live in.

July 4th, with another meaning... I wish I could be there with Cassie on her birthday... and the present a friend was supposed to give her for me, apparently wasn't given. She, "forgot." I am very upset about that, but Cassie will understand I am sure. God, I am in love with her. Every day proves that even more. How sappy can I get? Because I'll go there. I'll spare any future readers.

So highlights of the day: the extra blister, the beautiful fire I sit by right now, the way we worked to keep each other motivated, the views, and even the simple fact that we are actually here doing this. We got a little frustrated at times, but every time Lake Tahoe comes into view I am equally amazed as the time previous and I feel the tension lift.

Then there was the "moonscape." I don't think a single one of us got through it unscathed. As we descended Relay Peak, the windblown snow created a landscape that resembled Interstate Highway 91 in the springtime, or the moon. It was blistered with potholes and craters. I have this new problem with pain in my arches, Steve rolled an ankle and fell through the snow into a post-hole waist deep, John twisted his knee, and Greg's right Achilles hurts. It was maybe a mile of hardened snow and the most difficult downhill terrain you could imagine. You could barely trust your steps because the snow would either give-way or remain a rock hard stable platform. The sun was so bright and everything so blindingly white... It was unpleasant to say the least.

I did get to live my dream today, though. When I was little I remember seeing a picture I my boot scout manual of hikers walking through a mountain meadow, with snow capped mountains towering in the background, and wild flowers growing all around. I wanted to experience that. It was the inspiration for a trip such as this. Every time I saw a picture like that I would get a sensation of anticipation and excitement that I only wished I could experience in real life, I wanted it and I am here. What a sight. That picture when I was a kid had more than a thousand words and in the context of that valley the word count could be endless. It made me feel so small, yet so big. That is why we are here.

The magnitude of its beauty almost physically moved me to the point where my injuries were temporarily forgotten, it was like morphine to my aching body. And to top it off there was an ice cold mountain stream running through it where we were able to freshen up and replenish our water supply, Tahoe Meadows I believe it was called.

Soon after we returned to the cover of trees, we approached Twin Lakes. More like Twin Ponds but I am sure they are bigger in the rainy season. Our first view of the larger sibling was spectacular. In the middle of nowhere was this body of water surrounded on all sides by a grassy gravel arena; further out the tree line made its border. Placed in the water were a few scattered boulders, seemingly perfect in their round shape like they had been rolled around smooth in a Goliath-sized stream long long ago.

We parked our hides on the awkward, out of place rocks and took advantage of the remarkable lack of mosquitoes with a welcomed bath! The water was quite warm. We also had a chance to do some sock laundry and wash our dishes from earlier that day. We got a bit lazy in the morning and were eager to get going. The socks we hung from our packs to dry. Nothing like fresh socks dried in the breathe of a mountain breeze! A quick photo opportunity and then we hit the trail again.

What also amazed me about today was the number of changes in terrain. We went from dense conifers, to rocks and snow, to just snow, to wide open fields to forest, and all with unbelievable views peeking through to Lake Tahoe. Aside from the aching knees and feet and shoulders and bodies... just being here makes it all go away. Now if I can just get some sleep, I'm so tired but can't seem to reach the drowsy point of no return.

We also had our first bear sighting this evening. John was the only one who saw it and for just a quick second. I wait for my turn but don't get confused, I'd like to see one... not encounter one.

What a long day and we aren't even half way through this trail. Just make it through tomorrow, that's what I keep telling myself. As this fire dies down and the light begins to fade, I'd say this is a good time to go to bed.

We have to keep in mind that tomorrow is the next one day at a time.

Chapter Eight - Day 4

At some point the thing that we wanted to do turned into the thing that we HAD to do. I think that by day 4 we reached that point. We began to crave, like a drug, the thrill you get after dancing on the edge of self-destruction, only to make it out alive, just to do it again. It wasn't the end that we craved so much, but the means to that end and the surprise that every day brought. Yeah it makes mothers worry and children cry but pain feels so good when it's over. And boy is it worth every step.

July 5th 2006   7:30 pm – Pacific Time

If you aren't the type of person to carry on, even after your body said stop long ago, then you shouldn't be out here doing this, yeah, I said it. Let's just say that we belong. What a tough group of guys. John has his knee problem, Greg has his Achilles tendon pain, Paul has a sore foot, Steve did no physical preparation what so ever for this hike and is sore all over and dehydrated, and I have my bubbling, peeling, oozy, infected blisters and my swollen joints.

Everyone has something to slow them down yet we are just about to round the halfway point. After tomorrow (when we hopefully pick up our package of food for the second half of the trip at the Tramway Market) we will be just a few miles shy of halfway. I am so excited, yet I can barely walk. The fried little cocktail weenies that are my toes are no match for my will to push on.

I wore my boots again today and invented a new way to keep my feet safe from the sweaty swelling that has been my demise.

I took out the insoles in both boots to make room for my swelling feet, leaving just the extra arch support I had in there. Then I wore double socks to cushion a little better. On my right foot, which seems a little bigger for some reason, I cut off the toe end of one sock to make room for the swelling and put that on my heel for even more cushion. It felt good to know that if the snow gets too deep down the road I won't have to suffer the cold and wet. We all know that wet feet are not the best to have with already blistered, festering infections, and that is honestly no

exaggeration. I am beginning to get very worried. But

whatever, I'll deal with it when we are done.

I was thinking to myself on the trail today and it was

rather calming to say the least. There are times when we have

nothing left to say and we are left to our own thoughts, until

those thoughts conjure up something new worth vocalizing. As

much talking as we do and we do a ton of talking, I have a lot of

time for thinking to myself here as well. I mean we are walking

for most of the daylight hours and the days are the longest they

will be all year.

I am remarkably able to put things in perspective as we

get through this. I've discovered that it's the little things in life

we all too often take for granted.

Paul gave a good example after I began to vocalize this

thought. He said, that "even just two weeks ago we would have

thought twice about sitting in the grass, we wouldn't want to get

dirty, now would we?" The right thing to do would be to go get

a blanket and spare yourself the humiliation and the "you have

doo-doo on your pants" jokes. Who cares? That conversation

was brought to the table as we were sitting on a pile of sap soaked sticks, eating summer sausage, wiping the grease on our pants.

People struggle every day because they have no choice, and in society there are unwritten consequences for your actions no matter what you do or how trivial something might be (even sitting on the grass). There's always something to think about. That alone can be a huge struggle. It always seems there is pressure to fall in line. Now I enjoy the luxury of being clean but look twice before you judge.

I am who I think that you think that I am, and right now I have never cared less about who "you" think that I am. Right now I am thinking so highly of myself. Read that again. It makes sense I promise.

Out here we are struggling. Not because we have to but because we want to. I was so tired today on that ten minute break that I sat down right on that pile of sticks and sap, and oh my god it was great. It was followed by a game of who can hit the tree with a rock. I didn't even care about the sap on my ass, I was content. All I cared about was that moment. Hopefully we won't take so much for granted every again. Hopefully we will have learned and continue to use the knowledge that we gain out here. I think the knowledge is that everyone needs to struggle with others, not only to be able to cope with difficult things in life that are uncontrollable, but also to appreciate the things that are counterintuitively, good. Appreciate the struggle. We can all spend a little less time thinking about what we think others think is good for us and more about what we know is good for us.

The next time someone points out the little things that are wrong with me according to some standard, I will much more easily consider it and/or shrug it off. There are bigger things to worry about, like following dreams and getting to your next check point in life. Now I don't think I would normally just go around sitting in sap and not caring... my pants bill would get pretty high, but you get the point.

Let's get away from these ramblings and get back to where we are right now.

Spooner Lake is where we are camping tonight and though we cannot see Lake Tahoe or the massive mountains we just emerged from, this valley is easily one of the most beautiful places we've been as of yet. It's funny to think that just two nights ago we were camping at a lake that still had ice on it, with snow all around and now we are 2500 feet below that point in water that is swimmable... even bathable! But I am too tired and too sore to even move at this point... that idea quickly passed. As long as my feet stay clean I am fine. We all can deal with the smell; it's coming from each one of us.

This is certainly a much more traveled section and I believe we saw some fishermen on the opposite side of the lake. Weird seeing people. Sometimes it can be pretty desolate.

I took a picture of Paul in only his swim shorts, knee deep in the water, and filling his water bladder for purification. Dusk created a beautiful pallet of colors in the background, though Paul was only recognizable by his silhouette. We've taken tons of pictures but nothing will ever do justice what we see right now.

This place will do something to you. That is the point of this entry. There's something that just can't be explained, something that I may have to leave here on the trail. I'll just have to come to terms with that. Maybe no one will understand. Whatever it is, it's made me realize that no matter what I ever endure there will always be something in the struggle that will make me happy. This place truly is magical.

By now in the hike we were all a bit overwhelmed by not only the pain and surprise after surprise after surprise , but the sights as well. Here we are, hardened and strong after just four days. It's hard to believe that this is the same group of guys that huddled around the fire passing out clubs the first night when we heard that coyote. At this point on the trail we could have encountered anything and been confident enough to face it. That is as long as we weren't ready to go to bed locked in the tent with trail mix when something starts to move outside, something big, something hungry.

Chapter Nine - Day 6 (Recap of day 5)

July 7th 2006   8:38 am – Pacific Time

Yesterday, another long day. Not too difficult as far as terrain, but a little over the top as far as my feet and their worsening condition. I never even got the chance to sit down and write in my journal. Well, maybe I had the chance to but in the middle of it, sometimes all you need is to lay still, close your eyes, and reflect.

Today we are taking a well deserved half day. We would go for the straight up zero day but we are afraid we might need the extra time in the end. It's 8:30 and I just woke up. Definitely the most sleep I have gotten yet. Maybe a total of 5 hours!!!

Once we got into town yesterday my stride seemed to quicken just a little. I was feeling good seeing though we were about to reach the halfway mark as well as pick up the package containing the supplies for the second half. We sent this to the

Tramway Market, addressed to ourselves as the guide book

suggested. Cassie and Alexis (Steve's girlfriend at the time) *said*

they were going to send us something as well.

The trail ended and we had to make our way through

streets (actual roads!) in order to make it to the next trail head.

A couple of the guys ran through lawn sprinklers as curious

neighbors looked on in pleasure and apparent understanding of

our joy. We actually added an additional 2.5 miles to that 165

total they told us about in the description, I guess they don't

count the distance between the trailheads in the total.

On our way through town we passed by a fire station

and they were nice enough to let us refill our water bottles. With

FRESH water! I downed the first one in about three and a half

gulps and was soon going for a refill. It was great to finally

have some clean water that didn't have the taste of iodine or

Gatorade powder and iodine. It was like heaven on earth.

Appropriate seeing though we were about to enter the town of

Heavenly.

Irony rears its ugly head when the town of Heavenly

turned out to create more hellish problems and disappointments

than anywhere on the trail. First, our package with the next 5 days worth of food didn't get there, and then slowly everyone start to get the "explosives" (or "upset stomachs" to say it nicely). I wonder if it could have anything to do with that greasy puddle water we drank the other day...

As far as the package though, apparently they don't deliver mail in this place. Everything goes to a P.O. Box and we were never given a box number! Basically our package is floating around somewhere in mail land right now, or someone is feasting on granola and Ramen Noodles. We even called the store ahead of time to confirm with them that it was OK to send the package. Maybe it was a convenient mistake for them to leave out the P.O. Box number. More business for them. Afterall, what choice would we have?

To make things a little better we did receive the package that the girls sent us. Thank you Fedex for delivering to the doorstep! We ate what we could. Cookies, candy bars, and other junk foods of pleasure then sadly we had to give the rest away.

I felt horrible doing this, it was such a nice thing they did but with the condition that we were in physically, there was no way we could have withstood the extra weight and most of it was junk food. That would have been bad for us to consume

anyways. The card that Cassie sent me though was worth the

weight, a good pick-me-up. I had to keep that. When it hurts I

think of her and it; a pleasant distraction. I think of her a lot.

We resupplied our provisions at the market, which was

essentially a Quik-E-Mart convenience store, so naturally the

expense was HUGE due to the apparent "convenience" of it.

With everything being so convenient and heavenly

around here we decided to scrap the night's dinner plans and we

ate at a restaurant/bar nearby. If anything it was a morale

booster. A steak and cheese with fries was a very welcome

friend, and with all the water we could drink! Clean water!! No

pond scum!!! Oh how we take that for granted.

I feel kind of bad, but the guy who uses the bathroom

after we got out of there... good luck. Let's just say we were

much cleaner coming out than going in. And ring around the

tub? Try ring around the sink. It was gross. Sorry guys for the

mess.

So we had the bartender fill all our bottles with CLEAN

water and then we were off.

It was dark by the time we found a place to camp. We

setup our tents, tended to our feet, and the plans were to go right

to bed. Then Steve and I heard a noise.

We stopped talking right away. It was definitely

footsteps getting close. No, paw steps. I tried convincing myself

that it was just a deer, but those steps were just too big, too

many sticks snapping per step. The look on Steve's face was

such horror! White as a ghost. The only thing I could do was

mouth to him to not say a word and I gently, calmly pulled out

my knife. Like THAT'S going to do anything to a giant black

bear. Then I saw it. The one night that I leave my trail mix in

the tent!

Every night we have been so good about making sure

our food and dishes were up in a tree so that the local wildlife

didn't feast on our scraps and snacks, and the one day where we

see the most bear tracks than any other, I forget my damn trail

mix! I remember seeing a Fox TV special that said bears like

peanuts. They also told you what to do if you are encountered

by a bear. Let me tell you, you don't even think about that crap

when it actually happens. You suddenly forget what they told you to do should you have a run in such as this. Though you are

trapped in a tent I guess it doesn't really matter anyways.

So the steps get closer, and then there was the sniffing,

followed by a loud exhale then sniff then exhale.... the peanuts

no doubt. We were dead and we both knew it, but I stayed

surprisingly calm, maybe for Steve's sake, I don't know. I am

usually pretty good in pressure situations. It's afterwards where

I break down like a little girl.

Closer to the tent, I can actually see a silhouette from

the light of the moon... that little girl is starting to come out. No

offense to little girls of course; it's a man thing.

Chapter Ten - The Reason

For as long as I can remember I have loved to be out in the woods, night or day, by myself, and with nothing or no one around. It seems a little strange considering that most people would rather pull their own teeth than be out there in the middle of nowhere with those unpredictable noises lurking about.

At night, especially on moonless nights, everything speaks to you. The background noise of the day is gone and everything seems to echo through the woods like it is the only thing that matters to be heard. The wind on the leaves, an old barn owl, and my favorite - katydids! Those little green bugs are the symphonic score of my youth. To a lot of people that stuff is torture; when they stare into the darkness they have no idea what is looking back at them and that scares them half to death.

Actually, in Connecticut, the scariest of all woodland creatures are the bobcat and the coyote. However, they're nothing to really worry about considering how scared of you they are. They might run away with your cat or your small dog, but they generally won't come near a human. Every now and then a black bear will be spotted picking through someone's trash or knocking over your bird feeder in the more wooded parts of the state, but that's a serious now and then. Needless to say there really are no inherent dangers in the woods of good 'ole C-T. Well, there's the West Nile Virus but nothing a little bug spray can't prevent. I guess we have the poisonous copperhead which I've seen once sleeping on a rock in the sun and the timber rattlesnake. The rattler is so rare in Connecticut that I don't know anyone who has seen one.

So then I lied, we do have dangers but your chances of encounter are basically nil.

In the summer of 2005, my friend Jason and I were having a campfire on some property owned by his family in our hometown of Windsor. It's a Christmas tree farm that we used part of to make our troop's Boy Scout camp back in the day. Troop 203 still uses it today even though Jason and his brother are long since retired from the scouts.

It was a clear night, however dark from the lack of moonlight. One of those nights. I decided that I wouldn't have a problem being the one to go get the marshmallow sticks for the ladies, what a hero. I knew just the tree about 200 feet from the fire.

I walked from the clearing into the densely populated forest of mostly swamp maple and grapevines, just outside the reach of the firelight... and then I heard a noise. For the first time in my life I was scared. I was really scared. The smell of the ripening grapes in late summer, wind blowing through the tops of the trees, everything became loud and perfectly clear to my senses. I don't know what it was, nothing was different, and I had been there a thousand times before, but all of the sudden I was overwhelmed with a serious case of anxiety.

I told myself, "you're crazy, it's nothing, you've been here before... yadee yadee yada..." then I took out my knife; just a little protection in case that Wile E Coyote decided to come up with a plan for my demise. It made me feel a little better I guess. But I was the hero remember? There's no way way I could return with no sticks and tell them, "sorry, I got scared, can one of you ladies get me one too?"

So I finally reached my tree and the branches were pretty high and green, which made them hard to break off, especially with a knife in your hand. That's when I had an idea.

I really didn't feel like cutting myself so I would just turn the knife around in my hand so the blade would come out on the pinky side of my palm, edge away from my body. Perfect.

Imagine these thoughts going through your head as you are terrified. It seemed sane at the time. I twisted and turned that branch until finally... it gave. And in the process of all that twisting and turning about, I managed to drag the brand new factory sharpened blade across the meaty part of my left hand, just below my thumb that was fisted around the branch. It was a nice and clean cut. Actually, I barely even felt it. Not until the blood started to well up in my sleeve did I realize it was more than just a scratch.

I dropped the knife and slowly, calmly walked out towards the fire and gently beckoned Jason to come and take a look. He was a medic in the army so I figured call for him. Once I got near the light of the fire I realized just how much blood there was. My skin tone seemed to completely change to red, with not a patch of its original dirty white complexion left. It cut straight through the muscle, making my flesh flower out like a dandelion in spring. I figured it would be a good idea not to startle anyone else with this scene straight from a horror film.

Well that didn't work. How could you miss the bright red dripping thing that it looked like I was holding? The night was officially over. Sorry guys.

Needless to say I forgot all about the real or imagined dangers that lurked about in those woods on my hike back to the fire. So it turns out, the only danger to myself that night... was myself.

A little crazy glue, butterfly bandages, and a lot of Maker's Mark whisky, this egg was put back together again.

A few weeks later I decided that it had been too long since I had been in the woods, why would I let myself get so unacquainted with something I loved so much? I decided to go for a walk to clear my head and get my wits back. It was calming, and I realized what I had been missing. I actually heard a pack of coyotes howling and yipping in the distance. If you put it in perspective and appreciate it for what it is, then you can see the beauty and then it becomes not nearly as scary as it first seemed. Unless of course they are yipping and howling in a circle around me.

At that point I decided to start looking for a journey. A multi-day distance hike, and no matter what it took I would make it happen. A year later, there I was on the Tahoe Rim Trail, literally living a dream.

I think that's the problem with a lot of people, they are just too afraid of what they don't know, and that alone is what keeps them from enjoying things to their fullest. That reservation and fear may also be the one thing that causes them harm, not what it actually is that's scaring them in the first place, or whatever it is they are making up in their mind. Don't get caught up in your imagination; get caught up in where you are and who you are with. And always have patience with the now, you'll be happy you waited.

Now as far as things go that creep around your tent at night; there are certain things that will scare anyone, no matter how hardened and tried you are.

Then with a BANG! And a "HEY GUYS" from Greg... that's when my bowels let go. AHHH Greg you jokester! Or maybe another name that I can think of that would not be appropriate for all ages.

On the day we see the most sign of bears, and I leave my food in my tent, I have loose stool, and when I was the most tired.... But it was in good fun, I guess. That type of release is a common post sympathetic nervous system reaction. Fight or flight, danger over, then your body lets loose. I couldn't get mad at him; I know I would have done the same thing. I'll get him back. That breathing! I don't know how he did it but Steve and I were convinced that it all ended right there and then.

I was actually surprised at how calm I was during the whole ordeal, but afterwards, I just let loose. I was shaking to the bone. OK so I didn't actually crap my pants, but good thing I didn't have to go. And good thing we got to sleep in today, the morning after. Oh Gregory.

Chapter Eleven - The Donner Party

So our food never arrived, but at least we had a chance to restock for the rest of our trip. Yeah it sucked for us to have to go through something like that, but it always seems that somewhere down the line there is someone who went through just a little bit worse. It's good to understand that. It helps you keep a level head even when life might not be too even.

On our drive from the airport to Tahoe City our limo driver told us the story behind what was called the "Donner Pass" as we drove by. Don't get me wrong we're not talking one of those new state of the art, flat screen TV, light show, stretch, full bar included kind of limos; this was a torn upholstery, cigarette burn, 1970's kind of limo, with the box roof and driver in jeans.

The story was captivating but it also brought on a morbid thought of what could be coming for us. OK. Maybe not that extreme but when I got home I did some research to find out a little more about these people that were in such a state of struggle that they had to resort to eating their own people to stay alive. It was interesting to see the name of the same river we had crossed and the same mountains that made us struggle so deeply told in the story of the Donner Party.

For those of you who didn't pay much attention in American History like me, here's a way to at least appreciate what those light blue, short sleeved, collared shirt with a necktie teachers were trying to tell you in history class. No, I didn't like history all that much in school but this, this was different. I was standing in the middle of history, and about to make it myself. That makes it so much more interesting to me.

A lot of sacrifices were made to explore the new land that was the "Wild West." These adventurers trying to make their way to California where they were sure they would better off. The Donner party was just another of those groups looking for a better life.

~~~

"It's odd to watch with what feverish ardor Americans pursue prosperity. Ever tormented by the shadowy suspicion that they may not have chosen the shortest route to get it. They cleave to the things of this world as if assured that they will never die, and yet rush to snatch any that comes within their reach as if they expected to stop living before they had relished them. Death steps in, in the end, and stops them before they grow tired of this futile pursuit of that complete felicity which always escapes them."

~ Alexis De Tocqueville

The great migration to the west began in the 1840's when no more than 10,000 people lived west of the Mississippi River. Within ten years time, brought on by financial instability and diseases like Cholera and Malaria, more than 1 Million people made the trip to the other side of the river to find a better life.

On April 16th 1846 George and Jacob Donner, along with a man by the name of James Reed, set out with their families to lead a troop of 87 men, women, and children across a new way to the West. This "new" way had not actually been traveled yet by its designer; this man claimed it would cut the trip down and save time. They set out on a journey that would one day provide a story that proves the strength and the limit of human experience. It's almost like we are always on the move to find something more satisfying, something to keep the mind from resting, and in search of novelty.

Moving 10-12 miles a day, the beginning was easy. The Donner party made it to about half way and the tides began to turn. They lost nearly half of their livestock from attacks by the members of the Paiute native American tribe, in addition to those that went astray. Around the same time tempers began to flare, people started getting nervous, and one of the group's leaders, James Reed, had killed a man during a heated argument. Reed was banished from the group and they moved on. Leaving his family behind, he was forced to begin his own journey to California, alone.

The wagon train made its way through Nevada and it was said that there would be no snow for another month in the Sierra Mountains, but as the party reached the Truckee River (the Gateway to the Sierra) signs of winter were starting to rear their ugly heads.

It was October 31st and that night 5 feet of snow fell, that was just a glimpse of what was to come. What was left of this party could go no further. In all, there were 25 men, 15 women, and 41 children (6 of which were infants).

The snow continued to fall and slowly the food supply ran out. What was left of the meat was mixed with hides, bones, leaves, twigs, anything to make a meal. The snow began to drift into piles nearly 20 feet tall, and then the food ran out completely.

Weeks had passed and it was so cold and they were so starved, the party came to a consensus that one of their own must die in order to save the rest. The person who chose the shortest piece of paper would be the one to make this ultimate sacrifice. A man by the name of Patrick Dolan drew that fatal straw. No one could gather the courage to kill him.

The effect of the hunger and the hysterics finally took its toll and it is said that Patrick Dolan went insane. He fell into a coma and died shortly thereafter. It took some time but the hunger was just too strong. A man cut a strip of flesh from Patrick's arms and legs and he began to cook it over the fire. They hid their faces to hide their shame but this horrendous food revived them. It kept them going.

By this time they decided to set out a small party to find help. Shortly thereafter the party returned, with four of them dead. They wrapped their flesh and labeled it so that they weren't subjected to eating family. Three days later there was once again no more food.

They continued to live this way as the winter months rolled by.   As members of the party began to die one by one, their fate was all the same; they became nourishment for the rest. On January 17th, a month and a half later, the first rescue party arrived to find them buried in their snow shelters, nothing but skin and bones. There were half eaten bodies scattered around, a horrific scene. A woman with the flesh missing from half her body, her liver and heart removed, and her lonely dismayed daughter lying next to her sobbing, crying for Ma. But the rescuers were unable to take everyone. The rest must wait for the second rescue party.

After the second and then the third rescue parties arrived even more had been laid to rest and consumed. Of the 87 men, women, and children that set out on this trek to the west, 46 survived. The last remaining living member of the Donner party made it out on April 25th of that year.

It was to be the worst recorded winter in the area for the next one hundred years and nearly 6 months after being caught in the snow and 1 year since they first set out, the Donner party finally made it to California. Of the four Donner adults and the six children, only two children made it out alive, while every member of the Reed family managed to survive.

James Reed (the man banished for murdering a man) ended up the redeeming hero in this story. He made it as far as Sutter's Fort in now Sacramento, California and it was there he gave the information of his lost party. He quickly gathered a group of men for what was the second relief party. Not only did the Reed family survive this gruesome journey but they were the only ones to have made it without partaking in the horrible feast. They managed in other ways.

Until gold was discovered in this area a number of years later, the influx of immigrants in the west decreased dramatically after news spread around the country of this group that resorted to cannibalism on their impossible journey. Stories were told of the Donner party and how they grew to enjoy eating human flesh as they fought for survival in the Lake Tahoe region. Today, at the location of their camp, there are still relics

91

and souvenirs left over from this remarkable journey. And more so what was left is the story of an ultimate struggle and how it shaped the lives of more than just those involved. It eased the curious minds of hundreds of thousands of Americans across the nation; making them think twice about making the Journey. That is until the fever of the gold rush. Everything certainly does have a price.

~~~

It must have been good to finally know they could rest, after help arrived for the Donner party. Now I don't think I could eat Steve but we did get a day to rest, and what a difference it made. Nourishment for the feet so to speak… not feet for nourishment.

Chapter Twelve - Day 6

July 7th 2006   9:35 pm – Pacific Time

Though a short day for "recovery", a lot has happened.

Our original plan was to make today a really short day and

camp at Star Lake about 6 miles in, but once we got there we

decided to keep pace for just a little longer so we can gain some

of the lost miles we accumulated over the past 5 days. So from

Star Lake (which was beautiful by the way) we made our way to

Armstrong Pass.

One thing that I don't get is how there are fish in a lake

9,000 feet above sea level. I know there is no way these little

bastards swam their little fish asses all the way up this

mountain. Either they were put here by humans or eggs carried

by birds. Those two scenarios were the only we could come up

with.

So here we are at Armstrong Pass. A pass is a common

name for the space between mountain peaks which is generally easier to PASS through as opposed to trekking the summits. A

few miles back today we ran into a of couple of spunky Q-tips

(my name for old ladies with white hair) who said that they were

hiking in the direction that they were (opposite us) because they

heard this place was filled to the brim with snow. We were

getting a little worried and even tried calling the ranger's office

to find out for sure. With terrible cell service, all I got was that

there was snow and it would be tough for novices. He couldn't

hear a word I was saying though. Novice!?? Oh not us... we got

it! Not going to stop us! Then we got there.

And nothing. We must have gotten wrong information

or a miscommunication or something, because this place has not

a single patch of snow to be found anywhere. Just a beautiful

meadow on the edge of a swamp, and more bugs than anyone

could imagine. It is actually quite beautiful. I wish I was a little

more descriptive than just the word beautiful, but really this

place is just that. Good looking, gorgeous, stunning, dazzling,

astonishing, simply the most unpredictably fascinating place that

I have ever experienced. The way the sun moves through the

trees when you wake up in the morning. While the smoke from

the fire outlines the rays of that sunlight, the low hum and buzz of a tent zipper as everyone slowly emerges to start another day.

It's the smell of the thousands of wildflowers, the morning call of

the birds, the frogs at night, and wind blowing through the trees,

the feeling of tens of thousands of years of natural history and

the struggle of the hundreds who have been here before us.

After living in the suburbs of Hartford, CT my whole

life this is overwhelming. When I get home it will be total

sensory deprivation thanks to this place; and it's this I will long

for. And I can't imagine life without it... But there's no damn

cell phone service! If I wasn't worried about Cassie worrying

about me I don't think the cell phone thing would be relevant but

I am convinced she is convinced I am dead.

Talking about unpredictable; No matter how many

people we talk to or how many maps we study, we will never

know what lies ahead. That's another part of the beauty of this

place, the only idea that we have of what lies ahead is a few

lines on a map that represent elevation and what is within our

immediate view. It's challenging, we've hurt ourselves, we've

experienced "fire down below", no food, no water, wild life,

practical jokes, blisters, snow, desert... and we are halfway

through. A HUGE milestone! At this point I am more convinced

than ever that we will finish. As far as the map says, we have
one more really hard climb and the rest is looking easy...
Comparatively of course.

~~~

So right after Star Lake today the path was obstructed
by the outlet stream to the lake. John vaulted over fine with his
walking stick to use as a support, and I decided I saw a better
way. These logs that were laying across the start of the stream
(or what was the end of the lake) seemed like a no-brainer. They
appeared as though they connected on both sides and provided a
perfect natural bridge. Apparently they were not as connected
as would appear without closer observation.

The grass on which the logs were resting came up from
the water... not the land, and the logs were not resting on
anything, they were floating.

I got to just about the other end when the log I was on
began to sink. So I stepped to the next log over. That too sank.
Then I proceed to look in eight different directions while
stepping in time to the logs that gave-way under my feet. It was
like one of those video games where you have to move from
platform to platform without going under, or one of those crazy

Japanese game shows. One foot would go under, I would shift my weight and pull it out. It was like a life or death game of Dance Dance Revolution; all with a 30 pound bag on my back... it must have been a hilarious sight to see. I was pretty nimble I must say.

Just when I thought I was going to make it without getting too wet... let's put it this way, I had to change my socks before we moved on. Hilarious indeed, but now I only have one pair of dry socks. Let's just hope for a little sunshine tomorrow.

After my little dance party it was fairly flat, followed by technical terrain changes once again. As we rounded the base of the summit at Freel Peak, which is the highest point in the Tahoe region, it was desert like. A mile later it was dense forest. It is amazing how fast the environment changes. All the while around every corner is a new sight to amaze.

We saw changes in the vegetation as extreme as the changes in elevation. The bristlecone pines were my favorite. Their limbs were gnarly and their growth was stunted by the harsh seasonal conditions. They must have been hundreds of years old, their size not showing their age. (Fact check: actually, the oldest known bristlecone pine, or Pinus longaeva, is over 5,000 years old!)

Steve and I were having a great conversation along the way through this enchanting section. It seemed like everyone was a little more talkative than usual. The conversation was a little childish I guess you could say, but very meaningful to say the least. We were trying to figure out which Lord of the Rings characters we would be. No laughing we are MEN! That's what men talk about when cooped up for 11 days straight, doing something out of their minds to begin with. He came to the conclusion that he was Sam and I was Froto. Sam is a very loyal friend that will never let Froto down, while Froto always means well and does what he thinks is right no matter what. This meant a lot coming from Steve. OK I guess, pardon the geeky analogy but I like having these conversations with him. There was more to it than just the stupid conversation of what fictional character we most resemble; he was being real.

Steve is and has most definitely been that friend that will always be there no matter what. I don't think anyone gets him like I do and I am sure a lot of the time what he means to say (or do) doesn't come out exactly the way he thinks it does.

My main point is that throughout that conversation I realized that if he were just to try and be himself a little more he would be more understood by many; they would see what makes me love the dude so much. I also got to see a little of how he really feels about me. A lot of the time he is trying to "one-up" me or shoot me down, but I think he actually might look up to me in some-odd way, and that's his way of showing it. Thanks for always being there for me, and with me, Steve.

Chapter Thirteen - Day 7

July 8th 2006   8:46 am – Pacific Time

My determination is more than my pain, even though it's discouraging how bad my feet have gotten. I will lead the pack again today just to set the pace. I have to be careful and take care of myself and try to not go so hard like I did yesterday. I should also try and keep my feet a little drier; all that moisture just makes the infections worse. Day 7 here we come!

Just like there were times when we couldn't keep our mouths shut, there were also times on the trail where we didn't speak a word to each other. Not because we were angry or upset in any way with anyone; not even because we didn't have anything to say. Our minds were racing with thoughts, and worries, and pains. It hurt. Sometimes the best way to deal with the pain was to just stay silent. No use complaining, everyone hurt. No use getting upset about it, what could you do but take it all in?

The only thing you could do was put your head down so as to not trip on something and go. Then go. Then go some more.

There were days when we were so tired and in so much pain that we silently ate dinner, tended to our wounds, then went to sleep. I know there were times with me that I barely had the energy to write. Day 7 was another one of those days.

Someone told me once that you can use that liquid bandage stuff on your skin as a preventative for blisters. It worked... for a little while, but even a drip of water will eventually drill a hole into stone. All the steps we took each day in combination of sweaty, wet feet, nothing could have stopped the burning caused by friction. By this time in the trip I was used to the pain but getting very nervous about the potential for infection, which was beginning to rear its ugly head. But like I said what can you do? It's the price you have to pay for success. You can say my ambition is crazy, but at least this madman is fulfilled. And they will never, never be able to say I didn't live life to its fullest.

Chapter Fourteen - Day 8 (Recap of Day 7)

July 9th 2006   7:31 am – Pacific Time

I was just too tired again last night write. Yesterday was our 3rd longest day at 17-point-something miles. We are now at Showers Lake which seems to be a popular place to camp. There must be 50 people out here in the middle of nowhere. Families with dogs, couples, friends, some of these people I'm surprised made it here. Then again they haven't gone 100 miles or whatever it is before arriving. This is a great place to camp though. Clean cascading water to wash our dishes in and I even had the chance to clean my feet and legs.

We haven't been able to stop really and wash out of fear of the mosquitoes. Yeah, it's THAT bad. My legs were so dirty they were black. Oh no, that is no exaggeration either. I would wipe away a section and it was like washing your car after driving through the mud. I'm not alone on that one though either, everyone is pretty much filthy. We don't care though;

there are better things to worry about... bigger fish to fry. Up to this point I cared little for keeping anything other than my feet clean.

I slept a little better last night, compared to the total of about 2 hours I got the night before. My feet continue to plague me and my hips so sore it's hard to get comfortable. Though it's difficult, and every day seems to be more so than the last, when I saw that 100 mile marker yesterday it gave me great hope. Just 65 miles to go! By the end of today we should be in the Desolation Wilderness area and well on our way up the west coast of the lake, continuing the clockwise direction of our path to the beginning again. Looking at the elevation map, today and tomorrow should be our biggest climbs yet. We are almost there!

It continues to get harder and I continue the think about Cassie. As much as I don't want this to ever end, I can't wait to get home. To see her again is now topping the list of my drives to finish. Oh it hurts, but I need to finish this. Bittersweet.

Yesterday we had our first taste of rain. It wasn't too bad though. Just a passing thunder shower that was spectacular coming across the mountains, echoing through the canyons and valleys. One rumble of thunder would last a minute or more.

Towards the end of the day we walked through Meiss Meadow. HUGE! It was like out of a movie. Off in the distance as we broke through the tree line, our first view was of an old abandoned - what looked to be - a cowboy cabin or old farm. The backdrop to this scene was a steep wooded mountain side. We didn't get the chance to explore however. I was staggering like a drunk rabid raccoon, wobble legged with exhaustion and pain and wanted to just stick to the trail. We had another two miles to the campsite and at that pace it would take probably just over an hour. We are getting pretty good at gauging our steps to determine our pace and how long it should take us to get from point A to point B. We are often within 10 minutes, it's amazing what you learn when you are forced to pay attention to your world.

On the eastern edge of the meadow' before plummeting back into the woods, the Upper Truckee River made its way toward Lake Tahoe. We took off our shoes to wade through the rapidly moving water. Nothing like a quick ice bath to soothe the soles. We even took a few minutes for a photo opportunity. I snapped one of Steve then met him on the other side just to turn around and pose for my shot. What's an extra 10 feet out 165 miles?

It really was a beautiful sight, but so many mosquitoes. You would walk through a patch of them and they would follow you for miles. The little bastards finally found a large source of food, I wouldn't let it just pass by either. Steve looked like that kid from Charlie Brown that was really dirty and permanently engulfed in that cloud of funk, only that cloud was mosquitoes on Steve (and he, equally funky). Vicious little creatures!

Mosquitoes seemed to be yesterday's theme. You would swat your arm and literally kill 7 of them. The combo sunscreen/bug repellent wasn't so effective, I think they were mutants.

Along the way met two guys who were doing the trail in 8 days. Yeah, 8 days! That's about 20 miles a day. INSANE! My guess would be that they've done this type of thing before. They were a little weird though. I guess you have to be a little tweaked to do this anyways. I mean, people must think we are out of our minds when they pass us singing any song that comes to mind; some weird ones too. Anyways, with a little more sleep

last night, let's see if we can start this day.

Chapter Fifteen – Day 8

First of all I've never seen such enormous drifts of snow, no; I've never seen so much snow. Second of all I've never seen so many mosquitoes. Even better (or worse depending on how you look at it) I've never seen these two together at the same time. What hell the end of this day has been. This place truly is a foreign world. And there are so many unpredictable things, it makes this easily the strangest place I've ever been.

I remember back in my swimming days how it would feel at the end of a race. You never thought you had it in you; to keep going would mean certain death for sure. It's the kind of pain that radiates throughout your body and pierces through you while striking every nerve from the tip of your toes to the tip of your brain. You suddenly go weak, grit your teeth, put your head down and finish the race. Sit there for a second and courteously wait for the remainder of the competitors to finish before you get out (Should you be fortunate enough, of course, to have beaten them to the wall). It's polite but really it's just an excuse to catch your breath and recover before you move another muscle. Then, when the race is over you pull yourself out of the water, stand up (albeit slowly), and work your way to coach for the critique of the battle. When the meet is done you go home, eat enough for 10 men, go to sleep in your bed, and recover.

I thought I knew what pain was. I couldn't believe at this point that the human body, my body, could be pushed as far as it was going. To stumble into camp at the end of a 17 mile day knowing that over night you would get little to no sleep on the most level spot you could find. The spot that was still not level enough with a root up your butt, in a tight sleeping bag that is too short and nowhere near warm enough; with no pillow. Then you have to wake up the next morning at about 5 or 6 am, tend to your wounds and do it again. This is pain. But I think Greg says it best.

"That which is most precious, has to be worked for the hardest."

So true Greg. Greg's our motivational speaker, remember. He has always had a great way with words. Thinking about this further, maybe it's so precious because it was worked for with sick strain.

Lake Aloha. Wow. Helllo! That's it, that's all I could say. As we limped into the expanding view of Lake Aloha, where we would spend the night, it was becoming clear how this place got it's name. It's almost tropical here, only the water is just warm enough to keep from freezing. It's impossible to understand without experiencing this lake in the clouds how it opens up your soul. Surrounded on all sides by sheer rock face and snow, it's the perfect pot for melt water. And with the record snowfall they got here this past winter there's no wonder it's flooded. You can see trees that have long lost their leaves, drown in the blistering cold liquid. For a place this warm (consistently 85 degrees every day) it sure has a lot of cold.

Being 8pm when we finally park our rears on the comfy grey stone, it was perfect timing to watch the sun set between the mountain pass beyond the lake and witness the birth of the night's stars. Walking toward the day's final resting place, the shadows crept towards us faster than we could sounder towards them. The air was so clear and free of light pollution that the nighttime sky reveals far more to us than it ever would allow back home.

Right now we are waiting for Paul and John to return. They set out as soon as we got here (without their packs of course) to find a better, flatter spot to sleep tonight. There is what looks like a family about 200 feet from where we are right now that took the only good spot around the whole lake! Don't they know what we've been through!

That's OK though I'm getting used to it. Not like it will make much of a difference anyways. After we set up camp I had the chance to talk to one of the lake's visitors who was about my age. She said that her and her family had been here for a couple of days and they have been coming to this spot for many years. They usually did more hiking but Dad was getting older and it was getting more difficult for him to go so far. They seemed very nice. I hope I have the chance to do something like that with a family of my own someday, maybe even make it a tradition like they did.

~~~

Earlier today we stopped at Echo Lake. It is a recreational lake that sits itself tightly between two mountains, with houses and cottages along its northern shore. What a great place it must be to vacation... and it had a store! A "Chalet" actually. Fancy, I know. We stocked up on fresh water and had a quick ice cream cone for good measure. We read about this place in the guide book and we decided a while back, while at the Tramway Market, that we would buy some food at the market and some at the Echo Lake Chalet, it was appropriately named. We took the gamble and it paid off.

We were going to have the usual Ramen noodles and tuna or something boring like that but out of the corner of my eye as I entered the store... they had these two really big, really juicy Hillshire Farms Kielbasa and we just HAD to get them. For dinner that night of course, otherwise they would go bad. Oh my god they were good. We're really living it up out here with our kielbasa and Lipton Rice Sides. Out of nowhere Steve pulled out a couple of packets of Taco Bell hot sauce. What else do you have in that bag of tricks there, Steven? You holding out bro? Either way, that night we were kings. Kings of Desolation.

Desolation Wilderness is a portion of the Eldorado National Forest in California, and we were its royal family.

At one point as we moved through Echo Pass, around Echo Summit, another thunder shower rolled through, though it did not rain on us. Like the previous storm, the thunder seemed to ramble on for minutes at a time. It was actually quite eerie to hear it carry on for so long, even more so than yesterday.

So Paul and John just returned as I write this and it looks like this is as good a spot as any. We should get the stove going for dinner before we become dinner for these skeeters! Another end to another beautiful day!

Chapter Sixteen - Day 9

July 10th 2006   8:20 pm – Pacific Time

Dishes are for the morning! All I have left to do now is take care of my feet and write in my journal.

We had a quick dinner and ended up in our tents early, ready for bed. The mosquitoes were so bad we just had to get in the tents, we need our blood thank you very much. There are so many that they start to gather and form shapes like in the cartoons. I just think of of something like a school of fish that gets together and makes one big talking fish (in this case a giant mosquito) to better communicate with the traveler. Greg even wished at one point they would shape together so they could fight man-to-man; none of this sneak-attack BS. It's time to get into the tents.

Another fun nightly ritual we do before bed is the "find a tree for the bear bag ceremony." It's a matter of getting it up there and getting it to stay. I didn't think it was that hard, but it's fun to watch Greg and Paul fight over rope throwing techniques and which branch to use, so I leave it to them. That and the fact that by now I can barely walk let alone thread a rope through branches and hang a bag. It's amazing how a night's rest (even without much actual sleep) can get you ready to go the next day.

But here we are, another night with no cell phone service, and no conversation with Cassie. First of all cell phones on the trail are the true sign of a city guy, I figure it's for safety. We could make it without them, after all we are men! But when there is actually no way to even get a signal to use it, this means you are truly out in the middle of nowhere. That "can you hear me now?" guy from the commercials should walk his ass out here sometime and see what he gets.

I'm in so much pain right now that the thought of the finish line, Cassie, and home are the only things keeping me together. It's hard to move. I started out this day with such a negative attitude for the first time this trip. Usually I keep my mouth shut and let my pen do the complaining. I don't want to bring anyone else down with me. Maybe we all feel this way but it was to be the most difficult straight up-hill day yet and we need to do our best to feed positivity.

After the big climb, which was dulled by the amount of hype it was given, we crossed the high point through Dick's Pass. After finally cresting, the view of the lake comes back for the first time in a day and half. It was a very welcome sight; and then there it was. All that snow we kept dreading as we gazed across Lake Tahoe every day in the first few days, it has arrived. Not nearly as bad as we thought but on the other hand there was no path, no sign of a path, and no sign of a way around. The topographical maps can only show so much, and with a severe lack of trail markers, this is ridiculous.

So we looked left, we looked right, we looked up towards Dick's Peak, then we looked down... then we looked at the map again. It looked like the fastest, safest way to get to where we were going was one thousand feet below us, on our asses, on the snow. Yet another opportunity for sliding! We could have potentially bouldered our way across the snowy mountain side but the incline was so great it would have been far safer to control the slide, rather than have it come by surprise; that and it would have taken FOREVER.

It took some time to figure out that we should cut across to where it was most clear and slide down that way. There was a pair of tracks that lead straight across but if that was the two guys that passed us a while back, they seemed to be a little more prepared than us. They even had snowshoes and crampons.

Scott, the ranger we passed about 1 hour previous, mentioned that there would be quite a bit of snow and that we should probably have an ice axe or something to get across, and without the appropriate equipment it would be extremely dangerous. Seeing though we had nothing of the sort, we decided that sticks would do just fine.

In case we fell and started to do an uncontrollable slides to our death, our best bet would be to roll on our stomachs and dig in the 8 inch makeshift ice picks to slow ourselves down. Scott also told us that if worse came to worse we should roll over just the same and dig our elbows in. We are a bunch of hot headed tough guys so we went for it.

Greg was the first to take off. I never would have imagined Greg to be the one but there he went full speed across the mountain to our first point of decent, and let's just say the stick idea worked! Good thing he had them. At one point he slipped, fell, and about 200 feet down was a giant ugly pile of rocks just waiting to break his fall. But he dug his sticks into the snow, recovered, and moved on. Then we were next.

We made our way about halfway down (500 feet or so) doing this lateral walk/vertical slide method to avoid trees and rocks and hollowed out caverns in the snow from the melt streams below. Inherently dangerous I might add. The most dangerous situation I've ever been in now that I can look back at it.

So we get to about the mid-way point and we move from the alpine zone to where the trees begin to get thicker, taller, and more abundant due to the altitude drop. As the wind blows the snow around during a snowstorm, it creates a hollow, surrounding any object on the ground. When the rocks and trees warm in the July sun the snow around the object melts almost to the ground and a hole is formed. This makes it appear as though the rocks and trees were placed inside these holes by some crafty giant.

We got to the point where we weren't sure what to do. If you can imagine a gauntlet of pits on all sides of a narrow strip of snow. As out appears it is solid but we know that anywhere there could be a spot where the snow melted underneath, creating a trap just right for falling through and being buried. This was complete with a pile of rocks down below; it was a nightmare.

After a quick conference where we carefully considered our options, we came to the conclusion that there was really only one discernible and logical way down. This path twisted and turned down the mountain like a bobsled track and I was convinced that there was no way we could make it through without one of us getting hurt and without one of those fancy sleds. Thankfully I was wrong.

As I inched down a little to see if there was a better way (there wasn't) I hear Greg whisper to Paul, "may God be with us" and there he went. With a running start and a dive there he went sliding down feet first on his rear-end bobbing and weaving to the bottom using his stick brakes as a steering mechanism.

Now I'm not a very religious guy but that was a miracle if I ever saw one. After Greg carved our track, there we went one by one down the mountain for a good 100 yards at least. We even found that Nalgene bottles truly are indestructible. We watched as it tumbled to the bottom and clashed with the rocks below. This very easily could have been our fate.

This was simply the most fun I have had all trip, and we saved quite a bit of time at that. What a rush! We all made it unscathed to a point at which we were able to follow the lakeshore at the bottom until we met up with the path again. This far out in middle of nowhere there is a one in a million shot to find a trail marker, consider us very lucky today.

If there was a theme for the last two days it would definitely be "danger." That's one thing we were talking about on the path, once we found it again. Between the unstable snow shelves and the wet rocky down-hills there are so many ways we could have fallen off a cliff or through the snow to who knows where. What's more amazing is how we were able to slide down an 80 degree decline and a thousand feet of elevation and come out with only a few bruises. Oh and one bloody nose. Somewhere up there I got a spontaneous nosebleed for no apparent reason. Probably from the dry air, but that seems to be another problem of mine as of late. The contrast of red, spattered on white was surprisingly beautiful, artful even.

My day brightened a great deal after our sledding escapade. We cut a little time and from there on out it really wasn't bad terrain at all. Still pretty sore though.

I think what hurts the most is the down-hill. In the coaching world it's called eccentric movements, but in the real world we can call it the lengthening of the muscles to reach the next step below, while at the same time contracting as you lower your body weight, plus 30 pounds. Eccentric exercises can actually produce greater results in muscle breakdown and growth than other movements. Though not really what I am going for here. This, in combination with the balancing act to relieve pressure on my wounds, creates a pain from my ankles to my knees to my hips that is often unbearable and unavoidable no matter how hard I try. Also, in combination with the raw blistered skin on my hips from the support straps of my pack, it makes for a very uncomfortable night's sleep.

So we moved from no trees, through snow, through trees and snow, and now we are in the swampiest area we have seen yet; like a rainforest in a way and with more bugs than before.

What's funny is that even though I can barely walk, once adrenaline hits the system and you are set with a sudden wave of fear, you sort of forget about it.

I usually stay back with Steve to give him company and make sure he is not alone for obvious reasons, but I must have lost track of my pace while in deep conversation with Greg.

As soon as I passed a stream (that took forever to hobble across I might add, carefully planning my route) I hear Steve scream in the distance. Within seconds my pack was off and I was over that stream in two single bounds, running full speed across rocks and logs and anything else that stood in my way; like there was nothing wrong with me. After about a minute of this leaping and bounding I see him. Somehow he lost the path and ended up 100 feet astray, in a gully where he tripped and fell face first into the mud. He was OK but I started to feel the effects of the run. We made it back to my pack that I left with Greg, me with my familiar limp returning, and we were on our way again.

I seem to have a lot to write about tonight, but then again we are in our tents abnormally early this evening. So much daylight left to burn.

~~~

I'm starting to get tired but I have to mention these ants I saw today, I mean the killer ants I saw today. Not only were *they big, but they BITE! And there was so many of them, if I didn't move I could have very well been carried back home for dinner. I had to take off my shirt and shake it because I kept getting bit. I know now why they say these things live a military existence. They work so diligently to get their work done, and non-stop! You could see the path that they took to get back to their home, all the while carrying pieces of a fallen tree for whatever reason, food, building, who knows?! They beat a path across our path. I wonder how many little ant steps it takes to clear it out like that. There was actually a clearing, just dirt. I don't know, I thought it was cool.*

The final excitement for the day was Paul's genius remedy for my broken sunglasses. The frame broke and the lens popped out so he suggested using pine tar to glue it together. Genius is right! It worked! Well, it lasted the rest of the day anyways. I think I am S.O.L. for the next two days though.

But one more long day, a short one, and then it's back to Reno to get our reward. A night in the casinos, free booze at the tables, and a hot tub! Two more days, one at a time. It will be good to finally be able to heal... but let's finish first. Time to fake sleep.

Chapter Seventeen - Day 10: The Last Night

Greg –

"I thought we saw the worst with dehydration the first

night... I had no idea what I was getting into. There must have

been a dozen points when I was certain we could not finish,

when I was desperate to turn back or in too much pain to look

around me at the awesome surroundings. This was not tough. It

was impossible. But through the encouragement of the group

and taking it one day at a time we made it to the end of what

must have been the greatest event of my life. My greatest

challenge. And my first adventure..."

Paul –

"Dave, Impossible is nothing. Few will appreciate the

events of the last eleven days. Don't get angry or frustrated

when people blow you off or don't understand what went on over

here. You have been transformed. You have been forged in the

fires of the TRT, and have come out with a new definition of

challenge, triumph, and success. Cheers! We are new men and
are now in the possession of a new view on life."

John –

"Whatever doesn't kill me will only make me stronger.
This has been one of the greatest experiences of my life. I am
much stronger and there is nothing I can't accomplish without a
good group of guys and a solid walking stick."

Steve –

"Dave, I am very happy to have been a part of realizing
one of your dreams. I know what these trips are somewhat like,
but it was great to experience it with you. Honestly I didn't
know if I was going to finish this. I am so happy I did. I am very
much hurt physically but much stronger as a person. I miss
home, I miss Alexis. I miss real food! I am definitely very
satisfied, happy, and proud of myself to have finished this trip
with you. I probably would have not gone on a trip like this
again if you didn't ask me so excitedly. I'm glad you did. I've
lost a lot of weight. I needed to badly. I'm happy for that. I
want to try to keep it off. This was an extremely challenging

journey, physically and mentally, for the both of us. I'm so

proud of myself for finishing this journey, seeing it out to the

end, and to do it alongside my best friend... Priceless! Cheers

to a great experience!"

July 11th 2006   8:30 pm – Pacific Time

A lot of good things were said tonight after dinner by

the fire. We each said a cheer as everyone swallowed a

mouthful or two of whisky; a small flask that I carried the whole

way just for tonight. The extra weight was totally worth it.

There was a lot of reflection about the trip. Believe it or not 3 of

the 5 of us at one point admitted they were convinced they could

not finish. I believe it was the 5 of us, and no less, that kept this

party going. There is such emotion this final night. I think that

based on tonight's conversation we will all leave these

mountains something of ourselves and have learned that no

matter what we are faced with back in the real world, there is

not a thing we cannot face down one day at a time.

Today was probably the easiest... yet it was our longest at 20 MILES!! We decided to go the extra mile (so to speak) so we would be left with only 7 miles tomorrow.

The hike today was really a combination of the past 10 days we've been out here. We dealt with ups, downs, snow, sliding, swamps, deserts, sand, mud, mosquitoes, hot, cold, wet feet, burning feet... a lot can happen in 20 miles out here. On top of the fact that the terrain was more or less level, and slightly down-hill it was a great trek for viewing.

Minus my still growing foot issues and infections, I have found a way to focus on the goal that is so close now we can almost taste it. In the beginning of the day we set out quick, we were banging out 20 minute miles. That's 3 miles an hour, which may not seem all that fast but out here, injured, with 30 pounds or more on our backs, up-hill both ways... that's really good. We have gotten really good at judging our pace. We have gotten it down to the minute when we should arrive in certain places. It must have taken a billion steps to figure out, but we had the time; like a sixth sense.

We have all gotten so much stronger and everyone has lost weight like crazy. Some of which will be found again when

*we get the chance to properly rehydrate. Cassie will love this
new ass of mine I am sure... just kidding! Maybe. And a sore
ass it is.*

*My only hope now is that tomorrow will be a swift, safe
and DRY trip to the end of this loop. "The fellowship of the
rim" (another Lord of the Rings reference by Greg and Steve
today... geeks) will be completing their task! Oh sleep here we
come! ...if I can with all this excitement.*

Chapter Eighteen - Autobiography in a nutshell

It's amazing how sometimes we try so hard to *not* be like our parents. How often have you heard someone say "oh my god, I've become my mother?" Or, "I will never treat my kids the way my father treated me?" I think too often we tend to look at their faults and do our best to never conduct ourselves in a manner that reflects that. But there is another side of that too, remember.

Think about all the good qualities you pick up, or what you can learn from those negative ones. We can't ignore who we are; we can only embrace what we have been given in our upbringings and with that, make the decisions in life that carry us forward. We can dwell on all the faults of our fathers or we can learn from them. We can blame our parents for our own faults or we can take life by the horns and make it work by celebrating the good things we've learned

I used to think about this a lot. I used to shy away from challenges and ignore problems, hoping they will just go away. I feel like I get that from my mom. I am sometimes very critical of people. I feel like I get that from my dad. I used to blame the fact that I was unorganized on my parents. "If only I had been given a little more structure when I was younger." I honestly believed that for a long time.

I think that gives a bit of insight on the person that I am. I may not be the most organized, or even the most thoughtful at times, I forget a lot. But I think I have embraced who I am and I work at my faults. I try to say hello to everyone I see, while trying to not be so critical. My cellphone has become my calendar so I can always know where I am and what time it is, it's filled the hole in my memory. I don't settle for the way things are. Everything that my dad put me through, I learned from it. The times my mom forgot to pick me up after swim practice, I forgive that.

Forgiveness. I think that is the most important lesson of all. I think once you forgive, you can begin to learn and grow.

I used to be a really, really shy person. I was the choir geek kid with the big framed plastic glasses and the long hair. You remember that 90's cut? The long hair, part down the middle, shaved underneath? Yeah that was me. I hid behind that hair-do and those hand me down pants for so long. I never wore flannel shirts but I was pretty grungy. Luckily for the sport of swimming and diving I was introduced to a world outside my own, and my path to where I am today began.

I later became a diving coach at a Division I University. I didn't realize the significance of that my junior year when I began coaching at such a young age. My sophomore year was the last year the University had a men's program before it was disbanded, and then I decided to continue my career as the women's coach. I have also been fortunate enough to have been voted, 4 times, the Conference Diving Coach of the year.

I have a serious passion for what I do, and to be coaching at such a high level so young I feel privileged. I often joke that I am a psychologist first dealing with these college aged girls, but honestly there is very little in this world I would trade it for. I also consider myself a father, brother, and friend to them as well (but certainly not one that they can push over). For some of them this is their first real experience away from home. They need a place to turn where they can be themselves. I don't get paid very much either. In fact I began at a $2,500....

SALARY! Yeah that's what I made my first year there. It has gone up since then but I think it is proof of my passion.

Being a division I athlete is about working hard, struggling with grades and friendships, and missing home; and all while in the quest of excellence; for the chance to win a championship; for the chance to feel like you have accomplished something greater than yourself. Sound familiar? This long walk is just an extension of who I am, of who I have become.

I get that sense of adventure and the relentless pursuit of perfection from my dad. As much as I hated the way he treated everything like it was win or lose, or how he always used to make me feel like what I was doing wasn't good enough, I can appreciate a lesson that can be learned from that. Obviously, I have learned, that there is an edge you can fall off of, but I also learned that sometimes it's OK to dance on that edge; that's how you push that extra mile; that's how you succeed above all odds.

My mother taught me patience, compassion, forgiveness, understanding, and above all to be thankful for what we have. Ironically enough it was my mother who taught me to forgive my father. And through the admiration of my grandmother (her mother) when she told me how she respected the fact that I can forgive him. Obviously mom learned well from her.

Life is a cycle. You have to keep it moving, constantly learn, but never forget to stop and smell the roses. NEVER forget to stop and smell the roses.

I think that's me in a rather small nutshell. My friends may or may not agree, but I am happy with where I think that I am and there is something to be said from that. Especially considering how unhappy I was for so very long. Like I said before, you write your own future.

Chapter Nineteen - Day 11

July 12th 2006 …about 11:00 am Pacific Time

Lying here on this sandy shore of Lake Tahoe. Past my nose I see my feet, sand, water, and finally the whole of what we just walked. The Mountains that paint the background are bright enough to burn this image in my mind for I am sure the rest of my life. Everyone here at this, what seems to be a public beach, can see the beauty of this place, but I am sure that most will never FEEL the beauty like I do, and like my four companions do. At different points in the past few days we were a part of that painting from this view.

As we walked toward the end of our journey there was a serious increase in people, tourists no doubt, looking for a quick vista fix with a quicker exit back to sanity. Who would want to spend so much time in such a dreadfully dirty place?! From Tahoe City it is easy to get a piece of the incredible views this place has to offer. Even without traveling for days.

I look at it in a different point of view at this moment. The passing of cars the smell of restaurants; can you imagine the beauty of such a thing when you have been living on Ramen noodles, summer sausage, and oatmeal for the past 11 days? I can't believe the things that fill my senses, like the smell of pine in the air, the itch of the mosquito bites, and the view of two states from one glorious point.

We passed another duo of through-hikers that encountered us earlier that morning as we were breaking camp. These two young ladies and their dog that did the trail in 16 days! I couldn't imagine being out there for so long! One of them had done it before, so they said. As they waited for their boyfriends to pick them up at the trailhead in Tahoe City, they did a quick freshen up in the Truckee River. It was so crystal clear and inviting. We couldn't stop; we had just a few hundred more yards or so to go to return to the place we began this journey. Nothing was going to break our stride. My god it feels good.

I don't know what it is, and I have heard this before, but it's funny how your body and mind forgets pain and suffering to a certain degree, after the fact. It's almost like a safety

135

mechanism, to save your sanity. At the moment of our final steps

on the trail I could not for the life of me recall why I could have

possibly been in so much pain at any point.

We just finished, we were done, it was beautiful... and it

was sad. The bonds that were created here, will they last? I'm

going to miss waking up every morning, knowing that there will

be (by my side) four of the best friends a man can ask for to help

me get through the day and all the hard things in life that slow

us down. Then again I guess the simple memories and hundreds

of photos [and this book] *will be there as a constant reminder*

that, damn it, I can do anything. It feels so good it almost hurts.

Where can we go next year?

And so there was no parade, no Connecticut governor

to greet us, no Canadian Prime Minister, no news crew ready to

take our story as we crossed the final information kiosk at the

Tahoe City south trailhead. We had day dreamed during the

whole trip how it would be as we crossed the line and obviously

we got a little carried away out there, but it was good enough to

keep us going.

It was also good to hear the bustle of cars and the

round of applause from that group of mountain bikers when we explained to them what we just did. They were on their way up the mountain, opposite the way we came, to begin a guided mountain bike tour; something that would last maybe a couple of hours. The look on their faces gave me so much pride, they hardly knew us and they were proud of what we just did, what we just did... what we just did.

What we just did... without a doubt the most difficult, trying, mentally exhausting, and dangerous thing that I have ever done, and I have done some pretty stupid things in my time.

Today was a quick 7 miles on very easy terrain. I was quiet most of the time, leading the way, not even noticing the newly developing blisters on the balls of my feet from the sudden burst of energy that I had found; completely ignoring the pain that I had incurred on myself the past 10 days, or whatever it was. I was flying high! More so I couldn't believe it was finally over. I was torn. I know I will miss being out here with these guys but it will also be great to go home and start to heal; what an adventure.

I had so much time to think about my life the way it was, and I have come to 2 conclusions. First of all, I love Cassie more than I could have ever dreamed of loving someone. She's everything I have ever dreamed of and then some. Like a dream come true. The second is my health. I must find a way to keep myself healthy and in this kind of shape. It starts with eating the right things and exercising on a regular basis. No more of this every now and again stuff.

I haven't felt this good about myself in a very long time; minus the festering infections on my feet and the swollen joints.

My calves are HUGE! I just looked down and didn't even recognize my own legs. Maybe I'll start doing triathlons, Paul told me about one that our home town runs and we talked about doing it together.

Life is good. I have great friends, a beautiful girlfriend in and out, a supportive family, and all the drive in the world to be the best that I possibly can be. A little bit of struggle goes a long way; it makes you realize what it is that you have and how to appreciate it... another hour before our ride comes to pick us up... my thoughts right now are so scattered... I can't wait to celebrate in Reno!

July 13th 2006   12:19 am – Pacific Time

Ah Reno! Actually, it's nothing like the Comedy Central show but a good time nonetheless. After a very nice dinner at the Outback Steakhouse we decided to take a quick trip up to the roof of the hotel to bask in the hot tub by the pool where we gloated a little more about our successes and pains on the trail with a few middle-aged couples. Then, we hit the casinos. It was OK. Paul won 15 bucks off his first quarter then moved on to another slot machine just to win another $50 on his first quarter there! Lucky bastard! I played $60 on blackjack with Steve for about 2 hours and was up $60 at one point then they switched dealers and I lost it all. Damn you Anastasia! I will never forget you! ...All part of the game I guess. Steve on the other hand walked away from the table $140 richer than when he sat down. He always wins when I am around. Good thing I am good luck for someone!

Either way, I got a few free drinks out of it. The perfect end to a perfectly beautiful, ah... but painful trip. Home and Cassie tomorrow, enough said.

Chapter Twenty – The Final Entry

July 13th 2006   10:19 am – Pacific Time

Reno Airport –

So much has changed, and so much is familiarly the

same. I feel like this trip has done something for us all. While

working together it has given us the drive to be able to

accomplish something greater than ourselves. Everyone seems

to be bright and proud and eager to share their individual

stories... well all but Steve. He seems indifferent, but who's to

say what's going on inside. We will see if he intends to keep

working on bettering his health; and he looks good. He lost 15

to 20 pounds maybe. Me? I lost about 10 and am sure and mean

full well to maintain my shape. Perhaps gain it back in a

positive way this time. I wouldn't mind beefing up a bit.

There is so much I want to do with my life and the

means and ambition to do so start right here, right now. It's not

only about change, but positive change and it is so much more clear than ever before.   Anything is 100% possible no matter

what gets in my way. Not to say that there won't be pain

involved along the way, but at least now I know that tomorrow...

it's just the next one day at a time.

Epilogue

I understand that every generation has their issues with the day's youth but here's mine anyways. It is sad for me to observe people today and how there seems to be a lack of motivation in our "easy" society. Why work hard when you don't have to? "I deserve this" or "I deserve that!" I am here to say that quite simply, no you don't. Now, if you said you have "earned this" or you have "earned that" then maybe I would have a second listen. Entitlement is the attitude of a lot of people. And you know maybe it isn't a generational thing. Maybe it's people in general. Maybe these people have lacked the emotional ties to accomplishment and the drive to find time to just have fun; or even to work hard AND have fun. Like my dad said, "work hard, play hard." Everything had just become so easy and everything is automated. Or maybe they just honestly believe that what they are going through matters more than what everyone else in the world is going through. When you are given something, just because, does that really make you happy?

Maybe with such busy schedules most people believe it is impossible to find the time to do what makes them happy. I mean, the only way we were able to do this hike was because three of us were educators with summers off and the other two were in-between jobs. I'd like to think that most people have better control over what they do, but it seems this isn't the case. And either way, I don't think it is right to say you deserve something you haven't legitimately earned.

Amen. Hallelujah. And I am sure I have been preaching to the choir here. I think we all understand by now that there are controllable and uncontrollable forces that are around us every day, but we must find a way to overcome. It will without a doubt make us stronger and more prepared for our struggles. This is what makes us feel accomplished and proud.

To me, I deserved that cheeseburger I threw down the hatch in Tahoe City on our final day; because to me this hike was more than just a walk around a lake. It was the pain that told you that you were alive, the liberator from the cages of doubt, it was the glory, and the beauty. It is the fact that it provides a story to tell others who are in need of a pick-me-up, or even for myself to look back upon and realize that no matter how bad things get, they could be a whole lot worse; but either way you can make it through with the right words of encouragement, the right friends and support, and most importantly your experiences in life.

So no, my main point here is not that people are lazy. It's that a lot of people are lost because they don't see the good in the bad. They are brought down to the point where they've lost touch with what it truly means to live.

I set out to answer two questions with this book. One: how does the way people deal with struggle make them stronger, and two: what would drive someone to choose to do something as difficult as this? I think I found my answers. The answers are spilled out on every one of these pages; it's life.

We are animals, and animals love to play; like a cat with yarn, or a dolphin in the wake of a boat. And they like to win, or accomplish. The feeling of completing something so great is worth the struggle, and when you do, you will have the right to gloat about your accomplishments with friends and family (and anyone else who happens to ask "what did you do this summer?"). This is also where respect is born. Self respect as well as the respect of others.

If I were able to reach the attention of everyone in this beautiful, free country of ours and give them advice I would tell them this: Have fun, do something crazy, and for god sake get off your ass and live.

Afterward - February 2017

This past summer as the 10 year anniversary of this hike became a sober realization to me that life moves on, I decided to make finishing this book and actually doing something with it a priority in my life. A lot has changed since the five of us completed that grueling task.

In 2008 Cassie and I were all set to buy a house together. We were signing the paperwork when she had to sign an extra form. It was called the "exclusive right to represent" form. Our agent said that it was not important at this point, and that signing it was merely a formality. We were to read the whole thing then sign and date. Line number 4 stated, "upon being asked, you will agree to marry David Maliar." she turned around, a little bit confused, and I was holding a ring. Pretty sneaky, right? We had THE best real estate agent on the planet. Thank you Heidi.

While everyone was oooing and ahhhing, coming in from the other room to see what the commotion was all about and taking pictures, through teary eyes she said yes.

We were married on June 19th, 2009 and in November of 2011 our first baby boy was born.

Probably one of the saddest moments of my life was when I made the decision to seek different employment, as my job as a coach just wasn't going to cut it for our growing family.

I left my job with the University and when my son was just 6 months old I accepted a position as an Officer for a local police department. The next hardship I had to endure was the grueling 6 month basic training, only being allowed home on the weekends. I missed a lot of "firsts" with my son but it was all for him.

Had it not been for my trials on the TRT and the subsequent trials I endured in its wake, I'm not sure if I would have been as mentally tough at basic training. The physical and mental challenge was incredible.

The hike around the Tahoe Rim Trail had such a profound affect on my life. If there's a day that has gone by where I didn't think about the trip, I would be surprised. You could call it PTPSD, Post-Traumatic Positive Stress Disorder. I just made that up by the way. Every time I think about it I get an overwhelming feeling of pride and accomplishment.

It has had the same affect on all the guys as well. Greg and Paul have gone on to and continue to do amazing things around the world. John told me years later that he applied for a job and in his interview most of what he talked about was this trip around the lake. He got the job. Steve is now the chief operating officer for a small family company and is also doing extremely well for himself.

Since 2006 Paul and I have vowed to get out at least once a year with friends. Sometimes others can make it, sometimes they can't. Last year we did the 100 mile Massachusetts section of the New England Trail. We basically walked from New Hampshire to Connecticut through rural Massachusetts.

In 2014 my daughter was born. 15 months later my second son was born. It's been a busy 10 years.

Four years after my "retirement" from coaching I was able to work it out in my busy schedule to return to the University from which I started. I am currently working with some of the most talented and driven young ladies the University has ever seen.

Between my family, my outdoor adventures, my love for playing guitar and singing, coaching, writing, and everything else I manage to find time for I have become relentless at my pursuit of happiness, living in every moment. I mentioned in my journal that, in the end, at least no one will ever be able to say I didn't live life to its fullest. That rings more true today than ever..

If there is anything you get out of reading this book, I hope it is this. Be relentless. Don't be afraid to venture into the unknown. Surround yourself with people that make you be the best version of yourself and do what makes you happy. Be respectful. And above all, challenge yourself. This is the greatest means to strengthening your mind, your spirit, your resolve, and your character. And by the way, those thing lead to other successes as well, even financial success, if that is what you want. I also invite you to share with me stories of your struggle and how it has made you stronger. I think together we can be the change we want to see in the world. I truly thank you for reading and happy trails.

Tips and Tails From the Trail

The following is a collection of writings and short stories that I have a completed over the years to help others with their preparation for the big trip. All of the below recommendations are my opinion only and should be used as a guide, not a definitive answer to every situation. The best way to prepare is through experience. Like everything start small and learn from there. Best of luck and please feel free to contact me with your own tips and tales!

The Long Trail - 2015

I read an article online about a study that was done that listed the most boring towns in Connecticut. My town happened to be number 10 on the list. I was intrigued so I read on. Come to find out, I am contributing to the reasons for this sleepy town to having rounded out this distinguished list at number 10. The only criteria they considered was how much of the population consisted of parents and how many of the town's activities were extremely family oriented. The study essentially implied that if you have kids you are boring. I guess the Jersey Shore has become the only standard for an exciting life.

When I was younger and apparently more hip, the outdoors was my world. I was always scheming some kind of adventure. The exact opposite of boring, to me. Somewhere along the way that flame became dimmer, and to the point where a once a year trip was all I really planned for. Life got in the way. That's a great catch-all excuse.

Since my son was born, it seems that everything I do

brings me back. Everything has been reborn and everything I look at and do, I see from younger eyes. That brings the excitement back to me. This past year I have gone hiking, even just day hikes, more than maybe the last 10 years combined. My son is at the age (just turned 4) where he is starting to get his legs under him. You should see this kid go! He's like a billy goat.

We have a "special spot" that we climb up to on the Metacomet Trail that overlooks the Police Academy in Meriden, CT. He gets so excited about the wildlife, the views, "rock hopping," that it really brings me back to why I love to be out there. "Dad, I'm a really really good hiker, right?" You know it, Buddy.

So I put this all into perspective and here it is. My top 5 + 1 list of lessons I've learned on the trail this year. I did a lot of thinking while hiking the northern 30 miles of the Long Trail in the summer of 2015 alongside some amazing friends. This list is based on actual truth and experience, not like certain one way perspective "studies." So check it out.

1. Do, or don't. Everyone has something that they love to do.

You can either do it, or don't do it. Either way it is your choice. Don't make an excuse. Look at the "things" you do day to day and ask yourself if it is helping you, hurting you, or is it just passing time. I am absolutely sure if you look at it this way you will find ways to cut out the nonsense and make time for what you want to do, and who you want to be.

2. Surround yourself with "big headed" people. If people are bringing you down, holding you back, or just simply not on the same wavelength, then cut the ties. Or at least limit your interaction. My partners on the Long Trail are some of the most big headed people I know. But not in the sense that you would think, they are not full of themselves. They have big ideas, big dreams, and everything they do is big. We could probably solve the world's problems out there if given enough vacation time. We certainly find a way to solve our own problems at least and we truly inspire each other to do even bigger things.

3. Train, and live healthy. Here is a distance hike principal with real life applications. You have to be prepared for what is to come. Are you fit and healthy enough to embark on

this journey? Unless your aspirations are to be the best at video games and winning at Netflix marathons, then you have to be physically prepared for whatever you do. Constantly reevaluate your physical condition and make sure you are two steps ahead of where your daily tasks require you to be. You will enjoy whatever it is you are doing if you are not pooped and miserable halfway through it. Hiking is just an obvious example of this. Walking 10 miles a day in rough terrain with 30 extra pounds on your back will make you wish you worked out more often. Going on vacation to Martha's Vineyard and biking for the first time since you were 15 around the island all day, and being so sore and miserable you miss the whole next day, or worse getting injured, would be another wake up call.

4. Plan. Know where you are going and make sure you are prepared with the proper gear. Who knew that Northern Vermont in June would be so rainy, I didn't. I mean the trail was literally a stream 80% of the time we were out there. After a while it wasn't worth the acrobatics to try and avoid the puddles and mud so we trudged right through. Everything was wet, but my sleeping bag and extra clothes were dry. I have "dry bags"

for this sort of thing and thankfully I brought them. Plan for life as well. Make a list of what you want to do today, what you want to accomplish by the end of the week, where you see yourself next year, and what you will have ten years from now. Make that list and put it in your face. Stare at that list every day and then make everything you do every minute of every day a part of making those dreams happen. If what you are doing is hurting you, keeping you from those dreams, or delaying those dreams then cut them out of your life. Plan to succeed, or plan on getting comfortable in the rut.

5. Be forever "young." First of all, never let anyone dictate what is best for you. There is no such thing as one defined avenue for excitement and happiness. People are fulfilled in so many different ways. What you could take out of that article that bashed us boring mom's and dad's is that the young do have something right. Everything is new and exciting. It's your own fault if you choose not to see things that way. If you are in rut it is probably because you are surrounded by the wrong people or you don't allow yourself to get out and live. It's all about perspective. Have you ever looked at someone you've known

your whole life and suddenly noticed something new about their face? Now all you can see is that new feature and they look totally different. Everything in life is like that, you just have to look at it differently and suddenly what's old is now new. Now that's something to get excited for.

6. Whiskey. And finally, the number one rule of the trail: always have a little whiskey to share with your friends in the end. It's worth the extra weight. Tullamore Dew is nice, or a recent new favorite, Kilbeggan. Another single barrel Irish whiskey to die for. But moderation here folks, let's not get carried away. That's not good for you either.

Eat Like You Do On The Trail

Simple, Frequent, High Energy Meals for an active lifestyle.

Think like a distance hiker for a second, but it's Wednesday in the middle of your work week and there's not a trail in sight except for maybe a paper trail of memos and reports. Think about your meals; what you eat and how often. So you eat oatmeal in the morning with dehydrated fruit, maybe a pre-workout powder to add to your drink. There's a bag of trail mix in your cargo pocket for day snacking. I even saw two Appalachian Trail thru-hikers in Maryland eating peanut butter right out of the jar with a spoon while on the move.

Lunchtime hits, you want to eat something quick and not too filling because you will never get going again if you put yourself in a food coma. It takes so much energy to digest food it becomes counter productive to your daily activities.

A couple hours later, it's snack time and maybe you have a strawberry superfood shake, full of phytonutrients.

Then comes dinner. You want something nutritious, something with a little protein to help you recover and get going again for the next day on the trail. And throughout the day you are sipping on water from the tube that comes from your backpack. You don't even realize you've already gone through the 2 liters and now you need to search for another stream to filter a refill.

I might just be speaking for myself but why do we plan so carefully for a trip like this but when we get home it's back to convenience, overeating, and/or under eating. And water? I just can't remember to drink enough water! I drink more when it's hard to find and I have to filter it myself by hand.

Maybe that's the answer to my problem. The main reason I hit the trail is to feel human, to be in nature, and for the physical accomplishment when you reach that summit or trail terminus. We have to start treating every day like we have 10 miles ahead of us on foot with a 5000 foot elevation change. Now, I'm not saying that I think it would be right for you to pack a bag on Sunday before the workweek and carry your food with you through Friday, but planning I think is a must. The boss may not like that too much anyways, and it would be kind of strange if you always had a pack on. And me, I am a police officer. I already carry an extra 30 pounds of gear every day so forget that.

Fact: human brain development reached an astounding rate of growth when our ancestors began eating meat! That says a ton about what the protein and other vitamins and minerals can do for your health.

For the longest time I believed this was the ultimate argument for the omnivore diet. You crazy vegans.... I eat meat so I must be waaay smarter than you. Then I got smart and opened a book, or two.

The reason the meat eating thing made humans progress so rapidly, come to find out, is that meat is a dense, slow to digest form of food that keeps you energized and sustained for a longer period of time. As opposed to nuts and berries and whatever it was that you could dig up that day if you were lucky.

Still think I am defending omnivores? Fast forward to modern times. Go to a grocery store. Is there anything you can't find? Our society has solved the problem of food the shortage. We no longer need to fight for every meal. It is way too easy to get everything humanly necessary, and it's right around most corners or right downtown. You literally can get everything you need to live a really healthy life, full of energy and brain development simply by eating plants. In fact your body needs to work so hard to digest meat it makes your PH too acidic, and an acidic PH is linked to creating the perfect environment for cancer!

So am I a vegan. Oh hell no! you will never.... never get me to put down the knife. Never! I even built a huge smoker in my back yard with two, 4 foot racks so that I can treat myself and my family to the best damn ribs and pulled pork you ever had. Don't get me started on that.

I am a firm believer in a very non-strict diet that consist of whatever you want in moderation and everything you need. Exclusions: soda, fast food, and most processed crap. And don't get me started on that either.

So when I am on the trail this is how I eat. The following is an example of the average day for me and my companions on the trail. I will give you two recipes for each day just for options. Most of the work is done ahead of time, before we leave, and carefully portioned out so that we are all carrying our share, and only what we need. Sounds like the perfect way to live. Everything you need and no waste.

Try this for one month. Live like you do on the trail with high energy food, no waste, and plenty of exercise. I think you will be amazed at how you feel.

Breakfast:

Oatmeal. None of that quick instant crap that's half sugar. Real steel cut or Irish style oatmeal. Add honey for sweetness and dried fruit. I like cranberries. Also add a little ground flax seed to help with digestion and "regularity." One cup of this mix is all you need.

Pancakes. For one serving you will need:

1/4 cup of finely ground oatmeal (we have a really good blender at home that works great!)

1 T of ground flax seed

1/4 cup organic whole wheat flour

1 t of baking powder

1 T of honey

1/4 cup dried bananas

Mix all ingredients and add 1/2 cup filtered water

Coffee! Starbucks actually makes a really good instant coffee in a serving sized pouch.

Snack 1:

Have a bag of homemade trail mix with you at all times. Mix together all ingredients. Feel free to add any amount of any of your favorite nuts or fruit to this mix. This will definitely keep you going all day. Multiply this by 4 and you should have enough to ration out for the week.

1/4 cup peanuts

1/4 cup sunflower seeds (shelled)

1/4 cup shaved almonds

1/4 cup shaved coconut

1/2 cup dried fruit (just buy a mixed bag if you don't have a dehydrator)

1/4 cup M&Ms (because, what the hell)

Lunch:

We try to make lunch light and quick. If you can find a way to keep crackers safe (like an old Pringles can) then try this:

Cut 4 inches of summer sausage per person

3 inches of cheddar cheese

15 multi-grain crackers

Either be classy and cut a slice for each cracker, or just take a bite. We just take a bite.

Tuna fish: They make those sealed pouches with tuna that are a perfect serving for a great mid day meal. My favorite on the Tahoe Rim Trail was the lemon herb. You could even eat this on the go with a spork... right from the bag. It is much lighter than a can and way easier to open.

Snack 2:

In addition the all day snacking on trail mix, I always bring enough of a good quality powdered meal replacement drink. Look for a no dye, no added crap performance line that is great for extra energy and recovery on the trail.

Dinner:

First night: STEAK! We always marinade a big old honkin cut of meat and throw it in the freezer for the first night on the trail.

This way it stays cold all day and it is usually just about defrosted by dinner time. Throw in some asparagus and quinoa and you got yourself a meal.

Lemon Chicken and Rice:

I know they make canned chicken and have not seen, yet, a chicken in the pouch like I have with the tuna.... but maybe I need to look harder.

Find a nice long grain rice mix

Cook the rice with filtered water

Cook the chicken with cracked pepper and Himalayan salt to taste then add 1 t powdered garlic, and 1 t of True Lemon (a lemon extract). Cook until the chicken is warm.

Extra: There are always those nights where you don't feel like a gourmet chef and are just too tired. Stay away from Ramen Noodles please, and other high sodium low nutrient meals. I have learned this over time. They do make whole dehydrated meals that are pretty tasty and actually not all that bad for you. Chicken and mashed potatoes and beef stew are two of my favorites.

*Always stay Hydrated. A good way to gauge how much water you need a day is to take half your weight in ounces. For example I am 170lbs. half that... 85. I should drink 85 oz of water a day. Drink more the more active you are. Also a good gauge is to keep an eye on the color of your pee. If it runs clear you're good. If it comes out like orange/brown sludge like Steve on the TRT then it might be time to find a water hole. Stay away from sugary drinks like Gatorade and Powerade. They are great for electrolyte replacement but the sugar content is ridiculously bad for you. Water it down maybe by half or more and it should be good.

**Always bring a flask of whiskey for the last day/ end of the work week to share in your accomplishments. It's worth the weight.

***This is a pretty high calorie diet so be sure to stay active. A walk at lunch, a good workout in the morning or night, and stop watching TV.

The New England Trail - 2016

On the hundredth year anniversary of the National Park system, Paul and I decided to celebrate in the best way we knew how. We hiked a hundred miles of the New England Trail, a National Scenic Trail, through the beautiful state of Massachusetts. The weather was not very good for about the entire middle 50 miles of the trip. It also happened to be the most poorly marked section of the trail. This was one of those "I am glad we prepared" moments because we needed to change the plan.

The trail followed a clearing for the high capacity power lines, at times moving in and out of the woods for no apparent reason. We must have missed the turn off. After looping around twice and going down a mountain and back up we decided to just follow the power lines to the road where we were sure it would meet up once again with the next trailhead. The map we had was very complete except, of course, for this section and a few roads that we had to follow that were not named properly... but who's counting?

The day was getting long and with the ever increasing rain we were now keeping our eyes peeled for a good place to lay down for the night. Towards the end of the "trail" as we approached the road, we encountered some sort of camp. There was a freshly plowed field that was approximately 100 ft by 50 ft and what appeared to be a lookout tower, or a turret of some sort. An old cabin stood between us and a dirt road where a beat up old pickup truck sat unoccupied. This wasn't the most welcoming of scenes so we made our way back out to the power lines and around the property where we were met by an aluminum gate. Hopping over was a cinch but as I spun my other leg over to complete my semi-graceful traverse over this beast I caught a glimpse of the sign that was on the other side. A picture of a gun caught my attention first. Then the words seemed to jump out with a casual warning, "If we find you here tonight, they will find you here tomorrow." Point well taken. Lord knows what the crop of choice was going to be for this plot, but my feet weren't THAT tired. And I guess I really wasn't THAT wet.

We carried on and met up with the trail again, as predicted, and made our way to a very cozy spot for the evening. Welcome to backwoods New England.

The Planning Stage

"In preparing for battle I have always found that plans are useless, but planning is indispensable." - Dwight D. Eisenhower

WHAT!? What does that even mean? Well if you have ever been in the heat of a battle, or a hike, you know that no matter how much you plan you can never plan for everything and sometimes the plan gets completely thrown out the window. On the other hand having an intelligent and clear overall picture of what lays ahead is invaluable. For the Tahoe Rim Trail we began planning 6 months prior to us leaving. Some things like flights and length of trip are the easy things to plan. Some things are hopeful and never work out.

Once we arrived in Tahoe City, California we planned on catching a cab to the campground when they opened the morning of, where we had to pick up our permits for the Desolation Wilderness. We had to have these permits if we were to even enter the boundaries of this park. Guess what? No cabs. I f we had to walk there, it would have added an additional half day to our already late morning and we had 17 miles ahead of us planned for the day anyways. Luckily for us there was that bicycle rental place right there.

That's the benefit of planning. First of all we knew we needed these permits, and we knew where to get them. We just had to roll with a few punches to get them. So here is my process for planning for a distance hike.

Things to consider

Location - Depending on your knowledge and ability, likes and dislikes, time of year, etc; choose your destination wisely. You don't want to choose black fly season in northern New England, or drought season out west. Or maybe you do. I like to chose a trip that is just outside my comfort zone, but with this, ALWAYS have a bail out plan. Be smart. There have been many trips where one of us fell ill or we were just too broken to move on. Having to bail does not mean defeat, it means you live to fight another day. And sometimes it creates a story of its own.

Permits - Always check either the trail association website or documentation for whether or not you need permits. This is not something you want to do without. Places like desolation wilderness require this because, should you never come back, they know where to begin looking for you… Some places may require permits for other things like camp fires. Always check and please be respectful of the rules. I can't stress this enough. We all love these natural resources, please help preserve them and be responsible.

Maps - Go without a map, only if you don't have a family, friends, or a job to go back to. Just kidding, always bring a map. The best maps will show you potential water locations, camp locations, and are water proof! Topographical maps are the only ones worth anything and try to find one with an elevation profile. This shows a side view of the elevation gain and loss relative to the trail. This is a great way to plan your days based on how strenuous it will be. And besides, the last thing you want to do is plan on spending the night in a place that ends up being a bald summit. We had to stay one night above the alpine zone (no trees, just rocks) because one of our hike mates could go no further. (This might have been illegal but we were in a dire state and we left as little impact as possible.) It was a miserable night of non stop 60 MPH winds and pea soup fog. Not fun. And bring a compass. It's good to know which way is up when you get turned around and there is no sun for days. And don't hold your compass next to something metal.... I made that mistake before too.

Transportation - Are you doing a loop or a linear shot? Are you flying there and the nearest airport is 50 miles from the trailhead? These are things you need to consider. Some places run shuttles like up in the White Mountains of New Hampshire but some places are literally out in the middle of nowhere. What do you do? If it is linear maybe bring two cars and park one (with no valuables in it) on one end, then go back and get the first car in the end. Loops are the easiest because at the end your car is (hopefully) where you started. But often times you will need to rely on local transportation. Make these arrangements ahead of time. Uber is a fantastic option that I wish we had back in the day on more than one occasion.

One time we had to bail out early and I had to hitch a ride back to our car with a local who… let's put it this way…. He had a 40oz beer in his lap as he sped around town, taking "the shortcut." The beer was spilling in his lap as he told me one crazy story after another about his adventures on the trail. Half the time he didn't even have his hands on the wheel. I told him my name and tried to offer him some cash but he refused. He stopped talking to me altogether when I told him what I did for a living. He apparently doesn't like Police. He wouldn't even shake my hand. I shut the door and he sped away. Maybe he had warrants.

Food -

With water, this is certainly the most crucial part of your planning. You want to be sure you have enough food to keep up your energy, but you don't want to carry too much because pack weight is a pretty serious issue too. Follow the food plan included in this section and you should be fine.

Measure out daily portions ahead of time, and place them in individual packages labeling them with the intended date of consumption. This way you have little waste. Remember to always pack out garbage and extra food. Please don't be that guy or gal that trashes the place.

Food should be stored in a "bear bag" every night, strung up in a tree with a rope. Ideally you would like the bag 15 feet off the ground, 15 feet from the limb, and 10 feet from the trunk of the tree. Some designated campsites have a bear box that can lock your stuff in. Cabins are usually pretty safe too so you can keep your food with you in there. Just be careful of mice!

If you are planning a trip longer than a week I recommend scouting a location, usually a local country store or post office, where you can send yourself a care package ahead of time. This way you don't have to carry all of your supplies at once. Make sure you call ahead and get the whole address including any PO Box numbers! You can also take the opportunity to send home anything you don't need, like any gear you thought you would need and didn't.

Water -

You have a number of different option out there for water filtration and purification. I have tried most of them. From UV lights to iodine tablets to ceramic and charcoal filters, your options are endless. Bottom line, you need some way to clean your water because the things that you can catch out there can not only end your trip but could become serious in a matter of hours. Always have a backup too. I carry a personal water bottle with a rechargeable UV light that kills almost anything by basically scrambling it's DNA. It comes with a little screen filter too for the chunks. That is my go to. We also usually carry a filter of some sort and iodine tabs for a backup-backup. When boiling water, keep it at a rolling boil for at least five minutes to kill any illnesses causing microbes.

Please don't ignore your water levels. Always stop and refill when you have the opportunity and try to plan mandatory water stops based on major water sources located on your map before even leaving for the trip. We try to plan camp locations according to water availability as well.

Fires -

Now this is a skill that could potentially save your life. I have been known to start fires in the pouring rain with nothing but soaking wet wood and a piece of flint and steel. That's called "the man way." The other way is to use fire starter sticks and a lighter. Either way, bring both options and learn to use both efficiently.

Building a fire. Whether you are building a fire for warmth, or cooking, you should begin the same way. First is tinder (dried straw or grass, birch bark, small pine twigs, dried cattails, etc.). Next is kindling (small branches no bigger than half a pinky width). Work your way up from there, gradually adding larger and larger pieces in a teepee type formation until it is sustainable on its own. Prepare all of this before you strike your first match so that you are not hunting for supplies while it burns out on you. Basically, the secret to a fool proof fire is to start extremely small and slowly work your way up to larger pieces of fuel. With patience, this will work in almost any environment.

Please always practice proper outdoor ethics and "leave no trace." First, only burn sticks big enough to completely burn through. You only want to burn what you need to; no yule logs. If you can't break it with your hands or over your knee then leave it. No need to have half burned logs laying around everywhere. No one wants to see that.

When you leave camp you need to be sure that your fire is completely out and there is no trace of you being there. We don't want to see a million fire scars littered about the woods. If possible use an existing ring. And if the park regulations forbid it, don't do it. Camp fires are great but not at the expense of future enjoyment. You never know the reason behind the regulation so don't assume. Just obey, or go somewhere else.

Visit the Leave No Trace Center for Outdoor Ethics for more information on etiquette and the proper way to cover your tracks and leave the place as pristine and enjoyable as possible for the next group. They are an amazing organization with the most noble of missions.

https://lnt.org/

Physical Preparation -

I recommend a good High Intensity Interval Training (HIIT) program beginning a few months prior to your hike. This type of workout efficiently builds strength and endurance as while working stability and balance. Coupled with a good 10 mile trip every weekend or so with a weighted pack, you should be ready to hit the trail. It is important to do a lot of eccentric movements when working out. This is a highly efficient way to build muscle and mimic the conditions of trail life. Eccentric exercises are those, like walking down stairs, where the muscles are lengthening under tension. An example of this would be slow controlled lunges on the way down and fast up. This is opposed to concentric movements where the muscle is contracting while under tension, like a bicep curl. A good mix of both is ideal.

Like in the sport of swimming, try "tapering" your efforts rather than not doing anything at all on the days prior to leaving for the trail. Keep up the intensity but don't do as much volume. This is to give some much needed life to your legs.

During the hike it is critical to implement a good warm up\warm down routine. The morning should consist of some sort of weightless dynamic warm up to include squats, lunges, high knees, butt kicks, etc. Followed by light stretching, gradually increasing your range of motion. Never, ever stretch cold muscles. This could cause way more damage than you think. If you hit the trail with your backpack on without doing any warm up, you will greatly diminish your performance and ability to go the distance. You will also do much to prevent muscle pulls, strains, and tears, so get it done no matter how silly you think you look.

If you sit for any length of time during the day, like at lunch time, repeat this dynamic warm up.

At the end of the day you will find it beneficial to do some light stretching of your upper body as well as your lower body. Don't hold stretched for more than about 15 seconds. Work all opposing muscle groups equally. For example, if you stretch your quads, then stretch the hamstrings as well.

When you get home, it may do you well to not pick up your same old workout routine right away. Give yourself a few days to recover. Continue doing the dynamic stretching every day first thing regardless of whether or not you are doing a workout. This will aid in recovery. Unless of course you have some sort of serious overuse injury, then seek a professional.

Animals on the trail - and I don't mean Fido.

By all means, bring Fido, but check the regulations to see if pets are allowed. What I mean are lions, tigers, and bears. Well. mostly bears in my part of the world. But wherever you are do a little research to see what types of animals or other pests are in the area. "Grizzly bears, black bears, panda bears, spiders, scorpions, snakes, black flies, OH MY!" is more like it. Learn what to do just in case. If there are rattlesnakes, consider bringing the appropriate snake bite kit. If it is black fly season consider writing a will and saying goodbye to your family. Alright, they aren't THAT bad, but they will certainly ruin your trip. There are hundreds of anecdotal remedies but none that actually work. I even had a guy in Vermont recommend wrapping a rag soaked in diesel fuel around your head. I don't think I'll be trying that one though. Be prepared. Even if it's overkill.

For bears, and other nuisance animals be diligent about the way you do your daily tasks. Brush your teeth and wash your dishes well away from your camp. Bears have an amazing sense of smell and are drawn toward these sorts of things. I've been woken in the middle of the night to a baby bear scream echoing through the woods. Not something you can easily recover from and just go back to sleep. If all it does is make you sleep better, you win.

Rules to follow: don't taunt animals, don't try to pet them, just leave them alone. Believe it or not, this advice is needed for some who think all animals are like kitty cats. I wish I could give you advice as to what to do during an encounter, but my legal team advised me not to. I actually don't have a legal team, but just be smart.

Gear -

When choosing the right gear, don't just go with what everyone else has or the cheapest, or even the most expensive. Do some intense research. Try this stuff on. Plan the hike first and determine what sort of things you may need specific to your location.

Sometimes the biggest baddest hiking boots are overkill when all you need is a light sneaker. Remember, I hiked in TEVA sandals for days on the TRT. I tend to just hike in trail running shoes nowadays, unless I am winter hiking where I will need something warmer with more protection. Always have a plan B in case of injury or blisters or swelling to the point where you can't even get your boots on, never mind tie them.

As far as sleeping bags, they make them for every occasion and comfort style. You might think you need the mummy bag then realize you just can't sleep in the thing because you are claustrophobic. Climb in the thing at the store if you can!

Tents are always a tricky one. There are so many. Just go with something light weight that is big enough for you and your pack. If there are two of you, go with a "three man" tent. Be sure to set it up and take it down a few times before you go. You should know your tent well enough to set it up in the dark with no instructions.

Pay attention to normal weather patterns for the time of year you are going. Always bring a rain jacket no matter what. Even if it is just to protect you from mosquitos.

Flashlights. I bring two. One of those coal miner ones that go on your head and one that that is hand held. Paul has a lightweight lantern that has a crank charger and a USB outlet that lets you juice up your cell phone or other gadgets. It is all about personal preference when you go out.

Weigh your pack before you go. Ideally you want around 30 pounds. Any more will be pretty tough and any less will require sacrifice. This is obviously relevant to your own ability too. The ultralight packers go as far as cutting their toothbrush in half to save on ounces. They are the bare minimalists who could go with a 15-20lb pack. That is just not me.

Always bring extra socks. Smartwool is best. And then pack one more pair than that to be sure. And when drying your socks by the fire, patience is necessary here. I have plenty of burn holes from hanging them just a little too close.

Things that would be nice? A lightweight wire grill top, a solar charger, camera, pedometer, a folding camp chair, a journal, and musical instrument (or not if you can't play, please). Think of the things that you really enjoy, that would make your life better out there and consider it. Just know these should be the first to go if you are meeting your weight quota. There is a fine balance between misery with it and misery without it.

My TRT Pack Checklist

On the night before or the days leading up to the trip, get together with your walkabout mates and do a "gear draft." Lay everything out on the floor and work together to make decisions about what to bring and what not to bring. Make sure that you don't have any unnecessary duplicate items and distribute the weight as best as possible. Be prepared to take on extra weight if needed. On the TRT the other's helped carry my load when I could barely go on. On other trips my pack weighed as much as 50 pounds because I took on the burden of a friend that needed the reprieve. It is the way it goes. Don't complain, don't feel bad, that is part of the experience. The following is my personal pack list for the TRT and feel free to use this as a model when preparing for your own trip.

Shareable Items:

- Food
- Tent
- Large First Aid Kit to include
    - Band-aids
    - Mole skin
    - Gauze
    - Medical tape
    - Alcohol wipes
    - Tweezers
    - Burn cream
    - Triple antibiotic cream
    - Reflective heat blanket
- Dishes - pot to boil water and reusable plates
- Biodegradable dish soap and sponge
- Small white gas stove with extra fuel
- Large community water bladder (for cooking/extra)
- Sun screen that is also a bug repellant
- Camera with extra memory card
- Lantern with crank charger and USB port
- Firestarter kit to include: a lighter, matches, flint and steel, and a drier lint/sawdust mix
- Needle and thread
- Extra ziplock bags and garbage bags
- Permits
- Maps
- Guide book (optional - study it at home)
- Compass
- Approximately 50 ft of lightweight/ high strength rope like parachute cord.
- Water purification systems - Filter, UV light bottle, AND iodine tabs just in

case. Always have 3

forms for backup.

Personal Items

- [ ] Frame pack - size suitable for your body type and your journey
- [ ] Compression sacks for clothes and sleeping bag
- [ ] Nylon bags for food (and for hanging food - "bear bag")
- [ ] Sleeping bag
- [ ] Sleeping pad
- [ ] Clothes - depending on temp and time of year. This list assumes summertime (85 degree average). All clothing should be quick dry and moisture wicking.
  - [ ] One pair of "zip off" pants/shorts
  - [ ] 2 or 3 short sleeve shirts
  - [ ] 1 long sleeve shirt/ sweat shirt
  - [ ] Rain jacket
  - [ ] Hat with visor
  - [ ] Sunglasses
  - [ ] 2-3 pairs of underwear (wash to reuse)
  - [ ] 1 pair of socks per day (wash if needed)
  - [ ] Hiking footwear
  - [ ] Sandals for camp or hiking
  - [ ] Quick dry swim shorts
- [ ] Toothbrush/ toothpaste
- [ ] Deodorant
- [ ] Toilet paper AND baby wipes!
- [ ] Personal med kit to include: personal medicine and pain relievers, a few band-aids, lip balm, and anti-diarrhea pills!
- [ ] "Dry" storage bags. Everything should be in a waterproof bag inside your pack, especially sleeping bag and clothes.
- [ ] Cell phone and charger
- [ ] 2X water bottles
- [ ] Camelbak water bladder
- [ ] A small amount of cash
- [ ] Identification
- [ ] Pocket knife
- [ ] Watch
- [ ] Personal trail mix
- [ ] Energy drink mix
- [ ] Journal and pencil
- [ ] Monocular

- ❏ Small quick drying towel
- ❏ Flashlight and headlamp with extra batteries.
- ❏ Ear plugs! For the snorers in your group. (and other scary noises)

Packing

There is actually a rhyme and a reason with the way that you should pack your bag! Some would just assume "get it in there any way it will fit!" But with a little thought, not only will you be more comfortable, you will will be so much more stress free. There is nothing worse than tearing your entire pack apart looking for your lip balm, or even worse, your VIP (Very Important Paper) in an emergency.

Balance, Comfort, and Convenience. That is the principal to follow here. With these few short rules you are sure to have a more enjoyable trip.

1. Bulky items that you may not need until you get to camp go first, they should cram nicely into the bottom. This includes sleeping bags, tents, and dishes.

2. Heavy items should go in the middle of the pack, the closer to your body the better in order to help balance. There is nothing worse than having a pack pulling you

backwards as you are trekking downhill. This included heavy food items, water, etc.

3. Quick access items you may need on the trail should go closest to the top. This includes first aid kits, rain gear, extra warm clothing, lunch food, etc.

4. Outside pockets should be used for items you know you will be using often like bug spray, sunscreen, lip balm trail mix, maps and compass, etc.

5. The outside loops and lash points are great for other bulky items that may not fit in the pack like a sleeping pad, tent poles, trekking poles, extra water bottles, drying socks!, etc. Used carabiners to clip on the loops for easy access. Be sure to lash or bungee down these items so they don't sway with your swagger.

The Ten Year Plan

Finally I will leave you with this. Any journey in life is about knowing where you are, where you want to be, and how you are going to get there.

We were on day two of the Long Trail in Vermont and lord knows what conversation came before or after but the topic of life planning arose. Paul and I were pretty deep into solving the world's problems I'm sure and the thought of what to do after retirement came up. Now keep in mind we have about 25 or so years to go...

Paul has a very detailed 50 year plan and he would like to involve me with some sort of social program involving the great outdoors. He will be the president of the United States someday, you see. Or at least the Governor of Connecticut.

Crazy right? Dream big nature walkers. Then come home, back to Earth. Right?

I don't think so.

Paul is the kind of guy that intends to do something, then, like a great chess player, has every move and potential obstacle considered all the way to the checkmate. This is the guy with two master's degrees from two of the most prestigious universities in the world. He speaks four languages fluently, including Chinese, French, Spanish, and English.

He has done great work around the world doing things such as helping restructure the educational system in Haiti. It's all part of the plan.

So to say the least, this conversation had a profound impact on my life. When I got home, I began working on my own detailed future plan. I decided however to tone it down slightly, by about 40 years, and the 10 year plan was born.

This is so important to do as everyone has dreams that never get realized. What I hope to do here is outline my plan so that anyone can replicate it. It includes an explanation as to how exactly this plan will become reality.

A lot of people create dream boards. These are a collage of things they want, places to see, feelings to feel, and objectives to complete. The concept being that these things are placed in plane view for you to see every day, giving you the drive to work towards it. It keeps you focused daily on why you are doing the things you are doing. Work hard now like no one else, so that you can have the things later that no one else can have.

The problem with this method is much less a problem with defining your "why" and more a problem of "how."

Every year I have a major event that I would like to accomplish, such as in 2020 I intend to Summit Mount Kilimanjaro. With the passing of each year another year will be added to forever keep it at 10. It's posted so that I can see it every day. So I am constantly reminded of what I am working for. It is like the dream board, but it also has a "how." This keeps me on my toes and gives every daily task a meaning. Things to include in your plan are personal growth, family goals, places you would like to travel, business and financial goals. Also include, if you like, a few material objects that you may enjoy such as a vacation home, a boat, an addition to your home Etc. AND GIVE! Unselfishly find a way to give to, or give back to a cause or a person you love. This will only lead to even greater things; monetary rewards as well as (most importantly) intrinsic rewards. Great things follow great people.

Don't just list them, figure out how much they cost and what it will take to get there. This way you have a clear understanding of what you need to do daily to make it happen yearly.

There are goals and there are objectives. Goals are the big picture and objectives are the tasks necessary to reach that goal. Put more attention on the objectives that the goal. Set the goal, forget about it, then fall in love with the process.

In order to accomplish my goals, I will need an extra $110,000 in the next ten years. Sounds like a crazy and unattainable goal. But when you begin the break it down, it becomes a bit more realistic.

Here's my how! Cassie and I have started a home business that is growing every day. I am coaching on the side and all of that money goes into this account. I also do some personal training on the side. And I write. And... And.... And...

I have it worked out to the dollar, how much each think will cost over the next 10 years. Knowing this, I know what I need to do TODAY to make this week better, to make the month better, to make the year better.

Think about it. 110 grand equals an additional $11,000 dollars per year for the next 10 years. Everything you do should all funnel down into that one goal. This book, my business, physical training, believing, all related to one thing.

Honestly, I think that might be shooting a bit low as far as our potential when you break it down. Last year we we were up $10,000 in addition to our regular income. This year we should easily double that. We may get to some of these goals early. Regardless, I am ready to fight, you should be too.

We are not more fortunate than anyone. We were not handed a thing. How big is your head? Start by dreaming, then figure out what it will take to get there. Maybe you need to get out of debt first, maybe you are already working towards a goal. Once you have a plan, you have a purpose, and a person with a purpose is hard to beat. That is what it takes to accomplish your dreams, now go get them!

References

- Leave no Trace - Center for Outdoor Ethics

    - https://lnt.org/

- Tahoe Rim Trail Association

    - https://lnt.org/

- Connecticut Forest and Park Association

    - https://www.ctwoodlands.org/

- National Geological Survey

    - https://www.usgs.gov/

- National Domestic Violence Hotline

    - http://www.thehotline.org/

    - 1-800-799-7233 | 1-800-787-3224 (TTY)

    - Crystal Bay Visitors and Convention Bureau

        - www.gotahoenorth.com

- David Maliar's Contact Info

    - Instagram @strongerjourneys

    - Facebook @strongerjourneys

    - Email: strongerjourneys@gmail.com

91679141R00124

Made in the USA
San Bernardino, CA
23 October 2018